THOMAS ARNOLD
HEAD MASTER

THOMAS ARNOLD HEAD MASTER

A Reassessment

MICHAEL McCRUM

OXFORD UNIVERSITY PRESS
1989

Oxford University Press, Walton Street, Oxford OX2 6DP
Oxford New York Toronto
Delhi Bombay Calcutta Madras Karachi
Petaling Jaya Singapore Hong Kong Tokyo
Nairobi Dar es Salaam Cape Town
Melbourne Auckland
and associated companies in
Berlin Ibadan

Oxford is a trade mark of Oxford University Press

Published in the United States
by Oxford University Press, New York

British Library Cataloguing in Publication Data
McCrum, Michael
Thomas Arnold, Headmaster: a reassessment.
1. Warwickshire. Rugby. Boys' public schools.
Rugby School. Arnold, Thomas
I. Title
373.424'85

ISBN 0–19–211798–X

Library of Congress Cataloging in Publication Data
McCrum. Michael.
Thomas Arnold, headmaster: a reassessment/Michael McCrum.
p. cm.
1. Arnold, Thomas 1795–1842. 2. School principals—Great Britain—Biography. 3. Rugby School—History—19th century. I. Title.
LA2375.G72A766 1989 373.12'012'092—dc20 89–31649
[B]

ISBN 0–19–211798–X

Typeset by Cambrian Typesetters, Frimley, Surrey
Printed in Great Britain by
Courier International Ltd,
Tiptree, Essex

To my wife

PREFACE

Many have written biographies and other accounts of Dr Thomas Arnold, Head Master of Rugby School and classical scholar, so it might be asked what justification there can be for another. None of those, however, who have so written has aimed to assess Arnold solely as headmaster. None has had the combined experience of teaching classics at Rugby School, being a headmaster of two other major public schools, of being a governor of the school and married to the daughter of one of Rugby's more recent headmasters. With these perspectives, as one practitioner looking at another in the same field, I have tried to present not a new Life but a new slant to our view of his achievement as headmaster. It is after all his reputation as headmaster, not as ancient historian or religious controversialist, that has outlived him. Was it deserved? Furthermore his aims are still widely misunderstood, and I hope that my account of them, which deliberately sets out his published views in his own words, will help to correct this misunderstanding.

Inevitably, since Dean Stanley's full and famous biography is well known and, since it was first published in 1844, has been extensively quarried by successive students of his life and thought, I have not been able to avoid some repetition of Arnold's best-known remarks, but during the last thirty years much new material, some of it discreditable, has been discovered, notably by T. W. Bamford, so that our view of him has been modified. Moreover our view of what makes a good headmaster has changed too.

I owe much gratitude to many who have helped me, in particular Dr David Newsome, historian and Master of Wellington College, Professor John Roach, Emeritus Professor of Education, Sheffield University, and my eldest son Robert, of Faber and Faber, all of whom kindly read through my typescript and made most useful comments. They of course cannot be blamed for such errors and misjudgements as remain.

I am also most grateful to others who helped with various enquiries: Dr Niall Hamilton of Marlborough College who generously allowed me to read his unpublished Ph.D. thesis, 'A History of the Architecture and the Ethos of the School Chapel' (1985); Stuart Andrews, Headmaster of Clifton College;

Dr B. S. Benedikz, FSA., Sub-Librarian of the Special Collections at Birmingham University; Ms Naomi Evetts, Assistant Archivist of Liverpool Record Office; Mrs Jennifer Macrory, Librarian, Temple Reading Room, Rugby School; Sidney Miller, Head Master of Bedford School; Martin Rogers, Chief Master of King Edward's School, Birmingham; C. D. W. Sheppard, Sub-Librarian of the Brotherton Library, Leeds University, which possesses the largest collection of Arnold correspondence; Ian Small, Headmaster of Bootham School; and T. M. Taylor, Headmaster of Bromsgrove School.

Nicola Bion, Angus Phillips, and Hilary McGlynn, of Oxford University Press, having during the process of publication been most considerate guides. I am greatly indebted to Jill Cole, Madge Smith, and Ruth Wilson for typing various drafts.

Corpus Christi College, Cambridge. M. McCrum

CONTENTS

I

THE MAN

Unlike headmasters today, Thomas Arnold was appointed to his position without interview. To us the practice of relying on written testimonials unsupported by personal knowledge of the candidate seems strangely inadequate. Among the many testimonials of the more than fifty candidates[1] who applied for the Rugby vacancy in 1827 (possibly as many as a thousand if Mrs Arnold's family journal for 14 December reflected more than hearsay),[2] one, a letter from Dr Hawkins, Provost of Oriel, is said to have weighed most strongly in Arnold's favour. This contained the now famous prediction that, if Mr Arnold were elected to the Head Mastership of Rugby, he would change the face of education all through the public schools of England.[3]

Who was this young man of 32, so strongly supported by his referees that, despite his rather late application for the post and the fact that he was personally unknown to the twelve noblemen and gentlemen of Warwickshire who were the school's Trustees, he was nevertheless at once appointed Head Master?

Born at West Cowes in the Isle of Wight on 13 June 1795, son of a customs collector, he had shown early intellectual promise by his election to a scholarship, first at Winchester, then at Corpus Christi College, Oxford, and at the age of 19 to a fellowship at Oriel (which at that period had arguably the most distinguished high table in Oxford).[4] In 1819, at the age of 24, following his ordination as deacon in the previous year, he started his own private tutorial establishment at the village of Laleham near Staines. There for nine years, during which his wife Mary, whom he married in 1820, gave birth to six of their nine children, he prepared a small group of young men for university.

That subconsciously he may have seen this as something of a backwater is suggested by his writing in 1823, 'I have always thought . . . that I should like to be *aut Caesar aut nullus*, and as it is pretty well settled for me that I shall not be *Caesar*, I am quite content to live in peace as *nullus*.'[5] This inner drive he expressed more directly in a letter of 1826: 'I hope to be allowed, before I die, to accomplish something on education, and also with regard to the church.'[6] Later he confessed to being 'naturally one of the most ambitious men alive'.[7]

One aspect of his ambition was his constant wish to affect public opinion, on a whole range of issues far beyond his experience or knowledge. In November 1838, for instance, he was so much distressed by the agitation for more pay by those in the manufacturing districts of Yorkshire and Lancashire that he felt tempted to write: 'One man's writing can do but little, I know; but there is the wish "*liberare animam meam*", and the hope that all temperate and earnest writing on such a subject must do good . . . must lead men to think and feel quietly, if it be but for a moment.'[8] On another occasion, however, he showed himself aware of his lack of qualification for public controversy by writing anonymously. 'If I wrote by name in a newspaper published in another county, I should be thought to be stepping out of the line of my own duties, and courting notoriety as a political writer.'[9]

But his unambitious time at Laleham gave him the opportunity to indulge another less serious side of his character, his boyish love of energetic exercise.[10] Bathing and walking, especially in the company of the young, gave him pleasure throughout his life. Indeed the prospect of losing these relaxations in his new post was something he did not relish. As he surveyed his half-empty Laleham home, just before the move to Rugby, he wrote a farewell letter to the Revd John Tucker, saying how strong an interest he had in what lay ahead, '. . . the work I am not afraid of, if I can get my proper exercise; but I want absolute play, like a boy'.[11]

The word 'absolute' is a clue to one of his most striking characteristics, vehement and intense earnestness. Another letter (to W. W. Hull, one of his oldest and dearest friends) at the time of leaving Laleham expresses this trait vividly: 'We are all in the midst of confusion; the books all packed, and half the furniture; and on Tuesday, if God will, we shall leave this dear place, this nine years' home of such exceeding happiness. But it boots not to look backwards. Forwards, forwards, forwards,—should be one's motto . . .'[12] Bonamy Price, one of his Laleham pupils who later taught mathematics at Rugby before his election to the Drummond Chair of Political Economy at Oxford, described this dominant aspect of Arnold's nature well:

The most remarkable thing, which struck me at once on joining the Laleham circle, was the wonderful healthiness of tone and feeling which prevailed in it. . . . Dr Arnold's great power as private tutor resided in this, that he gave such an intense earnestness to life. Every pupil was made to feel that there was a work for him to do—that his happiness as well as his duty lay in doing that work well. . . . His hold over all his pupils I know perfectly astonished me. It was not so much an enthusiastic admiration for his genius, or learning, or eloquence which stirred within them; it was a sympathetic thrill, caught from a spirit that was earnestly at work in the world . . . a work that was founded on a deep sense of its duty and value; and was coupled with such a true humility, such an unaffected simplicity, that others could not help being invigorated by the same feeling, and with the belief that they too in their measure could go and do likewise.'[13]

The vehemence of language in which Arnold expressed his thoughts on the issues of his day was all part of this earnestness, his sense of urgency,[14] his feeling that there was no time to waste in putting the world to rights. His natural forcefulness, allied to a certain shyness in public, sometimes hid from others the humility that Price refers to, but that this was genuine is confirmed by those who knew him best. In writing, late in his life, to a recent pupil of his about life at Oxford, he shows both his own good opinion of himself and his essential lack of arrogance:

'I found, as my own mind grew, that those whom I had so reverenced were not so much above myself, and I knew well enough that I should myself have made but a sorry oracle. And this, I think, has hindered me from looking up to any man as a sort of general guide ever since; not that I transferred my idolatry from other men's minds to my own,—but as much as I have felt its strength comparatively with others, so also have I felt its absolute weakness and want of knowledge. I have great need of learning daily . . .'[15]

He did indeed work hard at learning, throughout his life, and had the benefit of a most retentive memory. At school and university he read widely, not by any means solely the classical authors. Aristotle was his special favourite, but Thucydides, Herodotus, and Xenophon were close rivals. For from earliest years history and geography especially fascinated him. Few schoolboys have read Gibbon's *Decline and Fall* twice by the age of 16. He also taught himself German and some Hebrew, and in his last years was trying to learn Sanskrit and the Slavonic languages. A strong intellectual curiosity was one of his most salient traits, as a letter of 1835 to a former pupil,[16] who was about to visit Asia Minor, vividly illustrates. In some detail he shows how much he longs to know on the one hand all about the geology, botany, meteorology, medicine, and agriculture, and on the other about its history, languages, and books. He urges the traveller to arm himself with Leake's map, a copy of Strabo's geography and of Herodotus's history, as well as a copy of Xenophon's *Anabasis* if he plans to go as far as Trebizond.

But, though he was intensely industrious, Arnold was human enough to admit, when on holiday in the Lakes, that he had found that the less he had to do, the less he did of anything.[17]

How far he was by nature authoritarian is, despite his critics, perhaps not quite so clear. It is true that he said of himself as early as 1817 (in a letter to J. T. Coleridge, nephew of the poet and a close friend from their time together at Corpus), 'I do not think I am democratically inclined',[18] and Lytton Strachey's picture of him as an awe-inspiring Jehovah figure is in that respect fair.[19] But most headmasters, if they are to be effective, are likely to appear authoritarian to their pupils. If a headmaster feels at all strongly (and Arnold felt passionately) about what is good for his pupils' education, this strength of feeling will probably come across to them as authoritarian. Arnold aimed to convince his pupils by direct teaching rather than by argument and discussion.

Nowhere were his convictions so strong as in religion. Although Lytton Strachey's iconoclastic study makes considerable play with the puzzled look in Arnold's portrait[20] and although correspondence with his friend Coleridge in 1819–20 confirms that early in life he had serious doubts about the doctrine of the Trinity, and reservations on three of the Thirty-Nine Articles, before he reached Rugby he had reached a settled faith founded on reason. Indeed, as another friend expressed it at the time, 'One had better have Arnold's doubts than most men's certainties.' The question supposedly asked by Newman in 1833, 'But is Arnold a Christian?', was misunderstood at the time and has been since, as Newman makes plain in his *Apologia*.[21] In the nineteenth century the word Christian was used to indicate moral virtues, especially selflessness; today it usually indicates belief in certain doctrines.[22] Newman used the term of Arnold in our sense and had some justification for doing so. But Christ was unquestionably all in all to Arnold. Yet to him the main value of Christianity was not its truth but 'the wisdom of our abiding by it',[23] a natural enough point of view in one whose cast of mind was practical rather than speculative. Goodness was more important than truth, for he was more likely to succeed in his aim of implanting goodness in his pupils than in convincing them of the truth of Christianity.

At the heart of his faith and of his religious and political thought was his attitude to the Bible. At a time when German scholars, by exposing its internal inconsistencies, had fatally undermined the traditional understanding that the scriptures are literally inspired by God, when geologists had shown that the Genesis account of the creation of the world could not be literally true, and when the growing respect for the laws of natural science suggested that their suspension by 'miracles' was, to say the least, improbable, Arnold in a series of essays and sermons showed that the Bible's historicity was nevertheless not discredited, nor its fundamental truth invalidated, by human errors or inconsistencies, by the consideration that every word was not literally inspired by God. While he regarded the case for the Bible's plenary inspiration as indefensible, at the same time his reverence for it and his determination to use it as a source of moral guidance were based on his belief in its fundamental historicity. As he wrote to H. H. Milman, 'it is a mere want of faith that impotently longs for the assurance of an imagined inspiration, and cannot be satisfied with that moral probability which exists in a human narrative when supported by the ordinary laws of evidence'.[24] He urged, too, the importance of interpreting the Bible positively with the aid of humanistic learning and laid stress on its primary value for ethical teaching.[25]

Looking at the Church of England in the light of the gospel, Arnold, not surprisingly, found it inadequate and longed to reform it. Arguing strongly against its disestablishment, he attacked the Oxford Movement on the ground that it would tend to bring about such an undesirable event, and he stressed that the Church must be reformed administratively so as to have a wider appeal and admit Dissenters.[26] He deplored the English clergy's habit of condescension towards the people, their liturgical preoccupation, and their exclusiveness, which drove many to Dissent.

Indeed there was no form of Church government which adequately represented the people's will. He believed as strongly in making the Church's constitution more popular as in broadening its terms of communion. He was ready to 'sink into nothing the difference between Christian and Christian' to win over

Dissenters.[27] If they were included in the national Church, 'great varieties of opinion and of ceremonies . . . while it worshipped a common God'[28] would be encouraged, or at least tolerated. This Church should be at once Protestant and Catholic, broad and inclusive. 'Of all our evils [in Christ's Church]', he wrote, 'the greatest [is] that men should call themselves Roman Catholics, Church of England, Baptists, Quakers, etc., forgetting that only glorious name of Christian, which is common to all, and a true bond of union.'[29] To create such a Church would involve a different concept of priesthood, changes in articles, creeds, and Church government, the use of different rituals to suit different congregations.[30] He was totally opposed to sacramentalism and sacerdotalism.[31] The laity should play a large part in governing the Church.[32] If the Church could be thus changed so as to meet the needs of the people, if the people saw that laymen were as much members of it as the clergy, that it was devoted to their instruction and welfare, and that it was not divorced from everyday life, they would not feel excluded. Arnold's belief that Christianity was fundamentally concerned with moral guidance enabled him to propose a type of Church that the Tractarians could not accept. His Broad Church liberalism, however, was unpopular with liberal churchmen and Dissenters also. The former were offended by his desire to include Dissenters in the Church of England and by the extent of his proposed reforms, the latter by his attack on their sectarian narrowness.[33] It was not until after his death that his ideas, far ahead of his time, gained some acceptance. Even today the role of the laity is far smaller, and the ecclesiastical hierarchy far stronger, than he advocated. Those in holy orders still have a predominant role in the Church's organization and management. Arnold's central belief that the Churches should vitally affect the ordinary lives of *all* Christian men and women has not had the influence it deserved.

His view of the Church was integrally related to his theory of the Christian state, convinced as he was that secular and religious matters could not validly be segregated, that life should not be 'cut into slices'. As he wrote to a pupil, the state is 'sovereign over human life, controlling everything, and itself subject to no earthly control'. It is divine and perfect, its essence is power, its aim human good. 'The State in its highest perfection', he went so far as to write, 'becomes the Church.'[34] In Basil Willey's words, 'for him the worst apostasy, the source of all woes, was the separation of things secular from things spiritual; this meant, on the one hand, the handing over of all temporal concerns to the devil or to the operation of natural laws, and on the other, the retreat of religion into priestly inutilities'.[35] Since most men achieve true happiness through spiritual enlightenment, the State's chief function is education, administered by the Church.[36] Social action, not dogma, would save the Church. As he surveyed the political and social anarchy of England, he 'became daily more reforming'. The ruling class must be exhorted to share power with the working class, the latter refined to wield its new power. But not too fast. He was a reformer, not a revolutionary. As Lionel Trilling expressed it, 'instinctively conservative . . . he saw that to conserve what he loved best he would have to change what he hated'.[37]

The distribution of wealth, for instance, was most unequal, but this inequality should be mitigated, not completely removed. 'Our business is to raise all, and to lower none. Equality is the dream of a madman or the passion of a fiend. Extreme inequality . . . is no less also a folly and a sin. But an inequality where some have all the enjoyments of civilized life, and none are without its comforts,—where some have all the treasures of knowledge, and none are sunk in ignorance, that is a social system in harmony with the order of God's creation in the natural world . . .'[38] A true and equitable commonwealth would come about when power was spread more widely among all classes. In particular, the working classes should have their bodily, intellectual, and spiritual condition raised, if not by individual and influential men of good will, then by the State.[39] In another letter to Coleridge, by now, in 1835, a judge, he wrote of the 'idea' of his life, 'the constructing of a truly national and Christian church, and a truly national and Christian system of education'.[40] Private benefactors should provide libraries and museums for those who could not afford to attend school, but these should be run by working men so that they would learn respect for public property. Middle-class education needed reform, too. The commercial schools were for the most part run by laymen and their curriculum was too vocational. The liberal education which the clergy brought to the public schools should be provided for the middle classes also. The idea of a secular education based on science, advocated by others who wished to improve the general level of education, did not have his support, for to him moral education in a Christian context was essential.[41]

He was a firm believer in the collective principle, and did not see, as we can see so clearly today, the danger in his remark 'I suppose the government may entrench upon individual property for a great national benefit'. Though he thought that the State should be the essence of the nation, he did not realize that the State was not yet that essence.[42] While he thought that there was an 'excess of aristocracy in our whole system, religious, political, and social', and that this had tended 'silently and unconsciously to separate the higher classes from the lower in almost every relation of life',[43] he did not discern what Disraeli discerned later, that England was split into two nations of rich and poor. Yet he showed exceptional insight into the social movement of his day. 'Now states . . . go through certain changes in a certain order,' he wrote in the first Appendix to his edition of Thucydides, 'and are subject at different stages of their course to certain peculiar disorders. . . . The popular party of an earlier period becomes the anti-popular party of a later; because the tendency of society is to become more and more liberal, and as the ascendancy of wealth is a more popular principle than the ascendancy of nobility, so it is less popular than the ascendancy of numbers.'[44]

But though he wished to improve the lot of the poor and took trouble to visit and talk with them in the workhouse or on the railway, and though he understood better than most contemporary observers what reforms English society needed, he did not see it as his role to advocate specific measures.[45] For he was diffident enough to realize the limits to his experience and knowledge. While claiming that political things were as real to him as things of private life, he felt more sure of himself beyond the British political scene, where he did not hesitate to make particular proposals.[46] Colonization, for example, engaged his close interest over many years, and he advocated it as a means of bringing the gospel to the pagan world, of promoting national commerce, and of reducing the population at home.[47]

His naturally polemical style in expressing these views on Church and State roused greater controversy than he desired or expected.[48] Though taken aback by the force of his critics' objections, he early decided not to embroil himself in publicly defending his position but to give explanation of it only to his close personal friends. With these he maintained a steady correspondence, and it is indeed from the contents of his many letters to them that so much of his views is known. The success of Dean Stanley's biography depends in large measure on the selection he made from Arnold's voluminous and wide-ranging correspondence and on the skill with which he interwove these letters with his biographical narrative. Several of the friends Arnold made as a young man at Corpus and Oriel remained close to him throughout his life despite their High Church and Tory sympathies, but perhaps closest of all in outlook, if not temperament, was Chevalier Bunsen, whom Arnold first met in Rome in 1827 as Prussian Ambassador to the Papal Court.

His second son, Thomas, described, in *Passages in a Wandering Life*, this deep friendship:

Never did I behold the passion of friendship better exemplified than in the feelings with which my father regarded that truly remarkable and gifted man. His German thoroughness on the one hand, and his ardent English sympathies on the other; his successful efforts to frame a comprehensive Protestant Church in Prussia, the very object which my father had so deeply at heart for England; the admiration with which both regarded Niebuhr and his historic method, and the deep interest with which my father (to whom jealousy was an unknown feeling) followed the labours of Bunsen in the field of Egyptology—all these and many other points of intellectual and spiritual communion constituted a union of souls seldom witnessed in this imperfect world.[49]

As late as August 1841 Arnold wrote to the Revd John Tucker, 'I scarcely know one amongst my dearest friends, except Bunsen, whom I do not believe to be in some point or other in grave error.'[50] Of all his friends' letters, Bunsen's were the only ones he did not burn as soon as he had answered them.

But, close as he was to his friends, Arnold was at least as fond of his family. As Archbishop Whately of Dublin said of him: 'He was attached to his family as if he had no friends; to his friends as if he had no family.'[51] In his first year at Rugby he had written to a friend that 'we live almost more quietly than we did at Laleham—hardly ever dine out, and see very little company', and this was so several years later.[52] But many of his and his wife's relations visited from time to time, and the domestic happiness that he evidently enjoyed is in sharp contrast with his public persona of polemical controversialist.

Mary Arnold, his wife, was a perfect foil, almost a mother figure, calmer and more stable. Nearly four years older, the youngest sister of his Winchester and Oxford friend, Trevenen Penrose, the child of a West Country clerical family, she seems to have provided him with the quietly secure home base that a man of such physical and intellectual energy needed. She shared his enthusiasms but was not so readily carried away by them. At Laleham they both found gardening a constant source of interest and delight, and together they visited the sick in the parish.[53] Later at Rugby, the daily afternoon walk beside his wife's grey pony at '4 m.p.h', occasionally accompanied by a Sixth-Form boy as well, gave both of them the fresh air and exercise they enjoyed so much and indulged their love of nature.[54] In the evenings, when he was free from writing or school business, he would read aloud to her for an hour or so, often from his favourite Herodotus, translating the book from the Greek as he went.

Many of their early years of marriage were of course, as with many similar families in the nineteenth century, taken up with the joys and anxieties of rearing a large family. Their nine children were all born by the time Arnold was 40, each nicknamed by him while still a baby—Jane (K), Matthew (Crab), Thomas (Prawn), Mary (Bacco), Edward (Didu), William (Widu), Susanna (Babbit), Frances (Bonze), and Walter (Quid). He dearly loved his 'dogs' as he called them, wrote family rules for them, and made time to be with them, sometimes teaching them himself, more often playing boisterous games. Stanley tells us of his 'cheerful voice that used to go sounding through the house [at Rugby] in the early morning, as he went round to call his children . . . the increased merriment of all in any game in which he joined . . . the walks on which he would take them . . . hunting for flowers, the yearly excursion to look in a neighbouring clay-pit for the earliest coltsfoot, with the mock siege that followed'.[55] In a letter of January 1841 from Fox How to W. W. Hull, Arnold describes taking all nine to skate on Rydal Lake, to their great delight. 'Four of my boys skate. Walter is trundled in his wheelbarrow and my daughters and I slide, for I am afraid I am too old to learn to skate now. My wife walks to Ambleside to get the letters, and then goes round to meet us as we come from the lake . . .'[56]

But family life was not all fun and games. Morning and evening prayers formed a framework to the day. Apart from taking a close personal interest in the subjects they were learning, he himself taught Latin to Jane and the older boys;[57] and he instructed all of them in swimming. To him they turned for information and advice, and 'a word of authority from him was a law not to be questioned for a moment'.[58] Many years later, his son Thomas was to write:

> My father delighted in our games, and sometimes joined in them. Stern though his look would be—and often had to be—there was a vein of drollery in him, a spirit of pure fun. . . . He was not witty, nor—though he could appreciate humour—was he humourous; but the comic and grotesque side of human life attracted him strongly. He gave to each of his children some nickname more or less absurd, and joked with us, while his eyes twinkled, on the droll situations and comparisons which the names suggested. In a sense we were afraid of him; that is, we were very much afraid, if we did wrong, of being found out and punished, and, still worse, of witnessing the frown gathering on his brow. Yet in all of us on the whole love cast out fear; for he never held us at a distance, was never impatient with us; always, we knew, was trying to make us good and happy.[59]

Yet that the fatherly pressure may on occasion have been too intense is suggested by Matthew's and Thomas's development of a stammer which was not quickly cured. Arnold, however, would not have understood how the pressures of family life in the home of one who was both headmaster and housemaster might have had such an effect.

From these demands Fox How, their Lakeland home bought in 1832, gave a much needed release for all. Arnold himself thought the countryside round Rugby monotonous and dull, 'beyond the reach of railways to spoil',[60] and never felt at home there.

> I care nothing for Warwickshire, and am in it like a plant sunk in the ground in a pot; my roots never strike beyond the pot, and I could be transplanted at any minute without tearing or severing my fibres. To the pot itself, which is the school, I could cling very lovingly were it not that the laborious nature of the employment makes me feel that it can be only temporary . . .'[61]

So Fox How, 'a mountain nest [of] surpassing sweetness',[62] meant all the more to him as the years passed. There he could find that leisure for writing which he longed for at Rugby. There he could enjoy family life to the full, celebrating his children's birthdays with enthusiasm, reading poetry or stories from Herodotus to them in the evenings, guiding long walks across the mountains. There, too, he could indulge his love of nature, which for him took the place of music and art, in which he had no interest or capability. The wild flowers on the mountain sides were, as he said, 'his music'.[63]

With so much in common with his neighbours, William and Dorothy Wordsworth, it is no surprise that a warm friendship sprang up between the two families. In the words of an old servant at Rydal Mount, the two men became 'terrible friends'. In the spring holidays of 1832 he mentions his 'almost daily walks' with William, and having a political disagreement only once, 'a good fight about the Reform Bill'.[64] Their presence at nearby Grasmere was one of the chief factors in persuading the Arnolds to buy land in the valley of the Rotha and build Fox How; Wordsworth's philosophy, as Mr Justice Coleridge, who had introduced Arnold to the works of the Lake poets, wrote after Arnold's death, 'brought out in him that feeling for the lofty and imaginative which appeared in all his intimate conversation'.[65]

Yet Fox How did not monopolize his holidays. Love of foreign travel took him across the Channel no fewer than twelve times between 1815 and 1842, often for extended excursions across Europe. His detailed travel journals, written for the benefit of his usually absent wife and family, illustrate his consuming interest in history and geography. The topography of each country was what fascinated him, and its relevance to its past history. He was no George Borrow, more a combination of Napier, churchman, and botanist, as his great-grandson Whitridge suggests.[66] Moreover, if not travelling in Europe, he was often visiting friends in the West Country or Scotland, and on these trips too he kept the same careful record.

The range of his interests and activities, only the most characteristic of which have been touched on here, was wide, so wide indeed that critics have charged him with inconsistency, if not hypocrisy. T. W. Bamford, for instance, points to some apparent paradoxes of his personality:[67] religious yet worldly; critical of pride and vanity in others, yet anxious for public recognition for himself; inspired by love and knowledge of the past, yet vitally concerned with the issues of the present; emphasizing the importance of law and order, yet in theory at least revolutionary; proud of England's political stability based on a firm hierarchy of classes, yet championing the rights of the lower classes; enjoying a gentleman's style of living though at the same time denouncing it as sinful; concerned with the preparation of boys for the professions which he openly despised. Other paradoxes of his character, as noted by E. C. Mack,[68] show him as 'tyrannical and gentle, dogmatic and enlightened, conservative and liberal, a man of principle and an opportunist, an idealist and a practical realist'. Although intellectually a liberal, he was indeed conservative by temperament, yet all these were superficial aspects by contrast with the dominant features of that personality, namely his deep religious conviction of Christ's divinity, and the integrity and intensity that this gave him. In the remarkable sermon that Stanley preached in Rugby Chapel on 14 August 1842, the school's first meeting after Arnold's sudden death at the end of the previous term in June, charged with emotion as he was, he doubtless succumbed to hyperbole, but his description of a man who always meant what he said, of 'such perfect truthfulness of character, so deep and undoubted a sense of the reality of heaven and hell, of God and Christ, as pervaded his whole being', rings true. 'Here was a man to whom, with the liveliest sense of earthly happiness and with the deepest interest in all that is most exciting and attractive in all the varied pursuits of human life, the thought of God and of death was ever present.'[69]

2

THE SCHOOL

Rugby before Arnold was one of England's seven leading public schools. He did not create, only enhanced and secured, its reputation. As early as 1810 Sydney Smith's definition of a public school (in the *Edinburgh Review*) makes this clear. 'By a public school, we mean an endowed place of education, of old standing, to which the sons of gentlemen resort in considerable numbers, and where they continue to reside, from eight or nine, to eighteen years of age. . . . The characteristic features of these schools are, their antiquity, the numbers, and the ages of the young people who are educated at them . . . even if we include, in the term of public schools, not only Eton, Winchester and Westminster, but the Charter-House, St Paul's School, Merchant Taylors', Rugby, and every School in England, at all conducted upon the plan of the three first.'[1] R. Ackermann's *History of the Public Schools*, published a few years later (1816), included Winchester, Eton, Westminster, Charterhouse, St Paul's, Merchant Taylors', Harrow, Rugby, and Christ's Hospital in that order. These were the schools which had gained enough of a national reputation to attract substantial numbers of 'sons of gentlemen' as boarders.

Dr James, under whom Rugby's numbers rose from 52 boys to 245, had established its fame by the time he retired in 1794.[2] George III said of it: 'Good school, Rugby; good scholar, Dr James—very good scholar.'[3] Indeed in the time of Dr Wooll, Arnold's immediate predecessor, who built the main block of school buildings which still stand, the number of boys had risen to 381, a higher total than at any period of Arnold's headmastership, and surpassed only by Eton. Arnold's peak was 360 in his last year, and that with the help of the railway. By comparison, Eton, always the largest boarding school, had 612 boys in 1830 under Keate.

After 1818 numbers at Rugby began to sink and by Christmas 1827, in Dr Wooll's twenty-second and final year as headmaster, had dropped to 123. Two increases in fees, first to 25 guineas per annum, then to 30, may have accentuated the decline, but the school had become unpopular for other reasons. The actor, William Macready, at Rugby under both Wooll and his predecessor Ingles, said that the former did not make him work as hard as Ingles had, and was too indulgent, 'a good-natured, amiable, pompous little man'.[4] The two main complaints were that the rod was used too much, and too little was done to foster the Christian religion. It is probable, however, that these were but symptoms of the general malaise affecting the public schools in the opening decades of the nineteenth century. Their low moral tone, the severity of punishment, barbarity of behaviour, poor living conditions, and restricted classical curriculum were notorious. Parents who might have been tempted to imitate the traditional clientele of families who regularly sent their sons away to board looked for marked improvements before submitting their children to the rigours of these schools.

If the public schools were to survive, they had to be reformed. Arnold and other headmasters during the first half of the nineteenth century effected the most necessary of the reforms and the schools' reputation recovered. The moral and religious tone improved, the school chapel becoming a significant influence. The boarding-houses, hitherto run commercially by dames who had no pastoral responsibility for the boys they housed, were now entrusted to housemasters; discipline was better, partly as a consequence of a new style of prefect; mathematics and French became regular parts of the curriculum. By these measures public confidence was so restored that the demand for places grew sharply, not least among the middle class. Thus numbers in the seven leading public schools began to rise again, and other schools, both old foundations and new, were added to the seven.

How far Arnold was responsible for this revival is a major theme of this book. Does he deserve the acclaim which he received during the second half of the nineteenth century as the great reforming headmaster? Or was he simply a powerful personality who happened to be running a well-known school, with the result that he was given credit for reforms that were being introduced into schools generally and that would have been made in any case? These are questions better answered at the conclusion of this study.

As today, the schools influenced each other considerably. Dr James (1778–94) brought Etonian practices to Rugby; Butler, a boy at Rugby under James, transplanted many of these to Shrewsbury when he became its headmaster (1798–1836); Arnold himself owed much to Goddard's Winchester, and admitted publicly his debt to Dr Longley, Head Master of Harrow, and to Dr Moberly, Head Master of Winchester.[5] Who should gain credit for a particular innovation is often hard to identify.

When Arnold arrived in Rugby in August 1828 he found a small school of 136 boys in a small Midlands town of about 2,500 inhabitants in all. The school buildings were comparatively new, all built between 1809 and 1816 except the chapel, which came later (1820). All but the last, which was replaced in 1872 by a much enlarged building, survive to the present, though modified internally, and are as portrayed in R. Ackermann's *History* or as described by Thomas Hughes in his account of Tom Brown's first arrival—as seen from the Close, a long line of yellow-grey brick buildings in the Georgian Gothic style, with the Chapel on the west, the School House in the centre, and the headmaster's house at the eastern end, with its battlements and turrets. Behind it were the Quad, Big School, and sundry classrooms. In Tom Brown's day the hall of School House opened on to the Quad, 'a great room thirty feet long, and eighteen high . . . with two great tables running the whole length, and two large fireplaces at the side, with blazing fires in them . . .'. Tom was delighted and surprised to find that every boy had a study, about six feet by four, which he shared with one or two others. This was the Rugby boy's citadel, his own home. East's study, which Tom visited first,

> was uncommonly comfortable to look at . . . the space under the window at the further end was occupied by a square table covered with a reasonably clean and whole red and blue check tablecloth; a hard-seated sofa covered with red stuff occupied one side, running up to the end, and making a seat for one, or by sitting close, for two, at the table; and a good stout wooden chair afforded a seat to another boy, so that three could sit and work together. The walls were wainscoted half-way up, the wainscot being covered with green baize, the remainder with a bright-patterned paper. . . . On each side [of the door] bookcases with cupboards at the bottom'.[6]

At night the boys slept in dormitories: Number 4 in School House, to which Tom was allocated, was 'a huge high airy room, with two large windows looking on to the School Close. There were twelve beds in the room. The one in the furthest corner by the fire-place, occupied by the sixth-form boy who was responsible for the

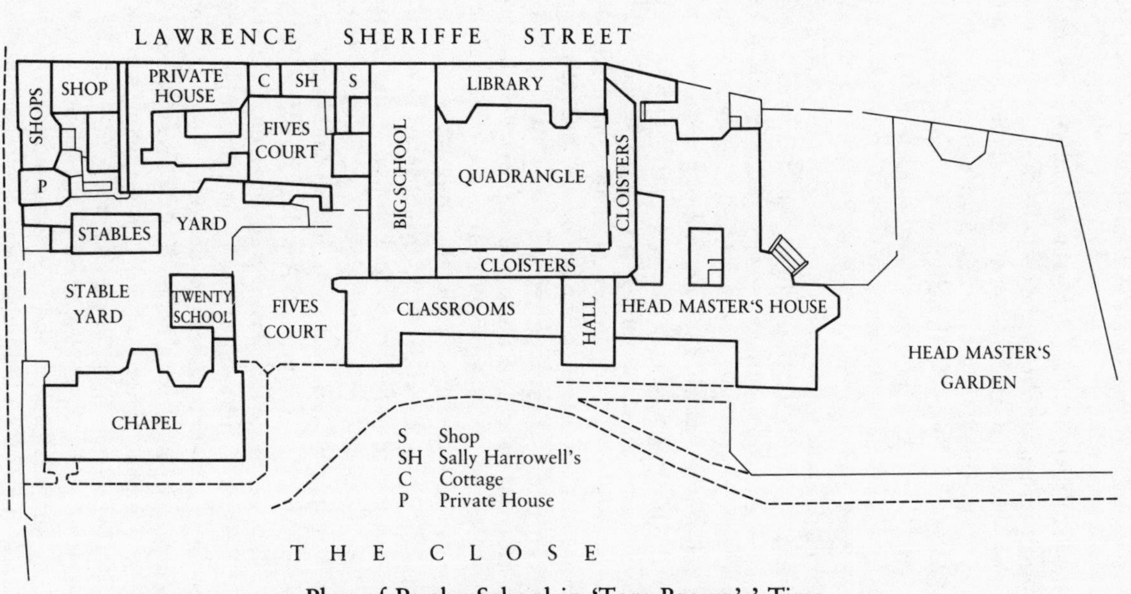

Plan of Rugby School in 'Tom Brown's' Time

The school now occupies the whole of the site marked in heavy black, the 'New Quad' having replaced the houses, shops, and stables shown above.

From *Tom Brown's Schooldays*, ed. F. Sidgwick (London, 1913), xxxiii.

discipline of the room, and the rest by boys in the lower-fifth and other junior forms, all fags (for the fifth-form boys . . . slept in rooms by themselves).'[7]

At the outset of Arnold's Rugby career, the school was organized for work in six forms, taught by the six full-time assistant masters, all clergymen.[8] One of these helped him as chaplain until he resigned in 1831. There were also others of a lower social order who taught drawing, writing, dancing, and French. By 1832 the staff numbered thirteen in all, rising to fourteen in only three years (1836, 1839, 1841). Thus the staff–pupil ratio in the year of peak numbers of boys and masters was 1:26. By contrast the average ratio for public schools today is 1:11. However, the staff were not too hard pressed, since they were not as occupied with organizing extra-curricular activities as their modern counterparts. Arnold, it is true, as we saw earlier in this chapter, had introduced a significant innovation which gave his full-time assistants a more direct share in the general education and welfare of the boys, as the dames who had run houses in the town to provide bed and board for boys who could not be accommodated in School House were gradually replaced by masters. But the extra burden, though no doubt heavy in terms of responsibility, did not take up too much time. This incorporation into the school of boarding-houses was not unique to Rugby. At other schools, too, the same process was occurring, a development of considerable importance.

That importance can be understood by considering the numbers of boys who were not boarded at School House. With some 40–50 day boys (the Foundationers) and 60–70 in School House the school when 'quite full' (293) in 1839, had to find beds elsewhere for more than half of its pupils. Arnold himself, early in his headmastership, persuaded the Trustees to set an upper limit of 260 plus Foundationers.[9] This total of 300 or so he thought was large enough, as large a number indeed as he could regularly count on recruiting, especially in view of his policy of removing boys whose behaviour or academic progress were unsatisfactory. In 1835 he told Dr Longley that 'the limit was set too high, and I do not think we shall keep up to it, especially as other foundation schools are every day becoming reformed, and therefore entering into competition with us'.[10] It was not until the railway, completed in 1838, had been in operation for a year or so that the school reached its complement. Indeed from 1834 to 1838, when Arnold was

	Annual Intake	Midsummer *Total*	Christmas *Total*
1828		136	160
1829	96	190	211
1830	113	251	276
1831	106	297	309
1832	80	—	313
1833	89	314	314
1834	71	314	298
1835	76	306	289
1836	76	299	280
1837	78	284	273
1838	80	274	282
1839	111	293	312
1840	121	325	346
1841	124	349	360
(1842	145)		

Note: Figures for the annual intake are from the *Rugby School Register*, those for the Midsummer and Christmas totals from C. W. Radclyffe, *Memorials of Rugby* (1843), x. In midsummer 1832 no list was printed as the school broke up suddenly because of the appearance of cholera at Newbold. Of the annual intake in 1842, 54 came in the Michaelmas term after Dr Arnold's death.

embroiled in controversy and much criticized, the numbers were well below what was desirable.[11] From 1839 onwards, however, as the figures show, the school expanded markedly and Arnold had difficulty keeping control of the numbers. In October 1840 he wrote, 'We are sadly too full in point of numbers, and I have got thirty-six in my own form.'[12] By comparison the numbers from 1811 to 1821, under headmasters far less well-known, never fell below 270 and for eight years (1813 to 1820) were over 300. Only in Dr Wooll's last five years did the numbers fall below 200.

Until the railway made shorter terms convenient, the school year was divided into two unequal halves, Long Half consisting of 21 weeks from early February to late June, Short Half of about 16 weeks from early August to late December. The Long Half was 'too long a period . . . either for boys or masters',[13] and in 1835 Arnold suggested to the headmasters of Eton and Harrow that there should be three terms of more or less equal length. But this was too radical a change to be introduced into Rugby or other public schools in his time. Nowadays the argument is whether there should be four terms rather than three, but the interests and prejudices of most have become so entrenched and the English summer is so short, that the pattern of the school year will probably remain much as it is.

DAILY TIMETABLE IN 1839

Mondays, Wednesdays, Fridays		*Tuesdays, Thursdays, Saturdays, Half-holidays*
7 a.m.	First Lesson after brief prayers.	
7.45	Breakfast.	
9.45–11.30	Second Lesson.	
11.30–1.15 Mon. & Fri.	Extra Study.	No School after Second Lesson but extra work till dinner.
(12.15– 1.15 Wed.	Arithmetic.)	
1.30 p.m.	Dinner.	
After dinner prepare for Third Lesson.		After dinner till 3.30, play.
3.30 Third Lesson. Break of ¼ hr. before arithmetic.		3.30–6.00 Extra work.
5.30 Finish Third Lesson.		
5.30– 7.30	Tea, and walk with friend.	6.00–7.30 play.
7.30	Lock-up.	
7.45– 8.00	Prayers.	
8.00–10.00	Prepare for tomorrow's First Lesson.	
10.00	Bedtime.	

Sundays must have seemed to many boys drearier still.

8.30 a.m.	Prayers followed by breakfast. After breakfast, learn gospel and sometimes a psalm as well for First Lecture.
10.00	First Lecture.
11.00–12.00	Chapel.
12.00– 1.00	Walk.
1 p.m.	Dinner. After dinner prepare 3 or 4 chapters of Bible for Second Lecture.
3.00	Second Lecture.
4.00	Second Chapel. Tea.
After Tea till 7.45	Private time.
7.45	Prayers.
After Prayers	prepare for First Lesson on Monday.
9.00–10.00	Private Reading.

The daily routine throughout the year, summarized in a letter of E. H. Bradby, written soon after he entered the school in August 1839, shows clearly why boys and masters found the terms too long.[14] By contrast with the variety of teaching and other activities available to pupils in independent schools today, the nineteenth-century programme at Rugby was like the Warwickshire countryside as viewed by Arnold, monotonous and dull.

Other than the study of the Bible on Sundays, the small amount of mathematics mentioned by Bradby, and some French, the curriculum was almost entirely classical. The school was divided into nine classes: First, Second, and Third Forms, Lower Remove, Fourth Form, Upper Remove, Lower Fifth, Fifth, and Sixth. Except for the Sixth Form, these forms were all divided into three according to proficiency in classical literature, arithmetic and mathematics, and French. Thus a boy could be in the Fifth Form in the maths or French division, but only in the Third or Fourth in the classical. The bulk of his work would be carried out in his classical division. All three divisions in the Sixth Form included the same boys. In August 1837 Arnold established a new form for the twenty senior boys in the Fifth Form who were not ready for the Sixth, called the Twenty. Chapter VIII of *Tom Brown's Schooldays* finds Tom in the Lower Fourth, which numbered over forty boys ranging from 9 to 15, a mixture of big stupid boys who were not clever enough to earn promotion to the Fifth Form, a large group of mischievous 11- and 12-year-olds, and a few young prodigies of 9 and 10 who were going up the school at the rate of a form a half-year. The boys spent such part of their energies as was devoted to Latin and Greek on a book of Livy, the *Eclogues* of Virgil, and the *Hecuba* of Euripides, 'which were ground out in small daily portions'.

The Lower Fourth and all the forms below it were taught in Big School. There, too, they had to prepare their lessons under the eye of the masters of the lower school. This arrangement did not work well: there were too many boys and too few masters to oversee them properly. So behaviour suffered. Tom Brown, like others before him, found the temptations too strong. One incident conveys the atmosphere well: at intervals round the edge of Big School were the raised desks, rather like box-pews, which the masters occupied when teaching. In the area occupied by the Lower Fourth, one such desk in the corner, which had room enough for four boys, was an obvious attraction. But since the fights to occupy it led to disorder, the master of the Lower Fourth ruled it out of bounds.

This of course was a challenge to the more adventurous spirits to occupy it, and as it was capacious enough for two boys to lie hid there completely, it was seldom that it remained empty, notwithstanding the veto. Small holes were cut in the front, through which the occupants watched the masters as they walked up and down, and as lesson time approached, one boy at a time stole out and down the steps, as the masters' backs were turned, and mingled with the general crowd on the forms below. Tom and East had successfully occupied the desk some half dozen times, and were grown so reckless that they were in the habit of playing small games with fives'-balls inside. . . . One day . . . the game became more exciting than usual, and the ball slipped through East's fingers, and rolled slowly down the steps and out into the middle of the school, just as the masters turned in their walk and faced round upon the desk. The young delinquents watched their master through the look-out holes march slowly down the school straight upon their retreat, while all the boys in the neighbourhood of course stopped their work to look on: and not only were they ignominiously drawn out, and caned over the hand then and there, but their characters for steadiness were gone from that time. However, as they only shared the fate of some three-fourths of the rest of the form, this did not weigh heavily upon them.[15]

Though there was a good deal of corporal punishment, administered by senior boys as well as masters, 'lines', that is, copying out in neat copperplate Latin hexameters or similar assignments, was the usual form of punishment and was imposed for minor offences.

Out of school, according to young Bradby, the only games were cricket, football, and fives,[16] which were left to the boys to organize as they liked. He himself as a new boy spent much of his spare time walking with a friend. But doubtless, as he settled into the school, he would have joined in the swimming, fishing, and bird's-nesting expeditions described by Thomas Hughes with such nostalgic pleasure.[17] A mile of the river Avon was rented by the Trustees for the boys to bathe in. There, within twenty minutes' walk from the school, in ponds or holes of various sizes, such as Anstey's, six feet deep and twelve feet across for those who had just learnt to swim, or Swift's, 'ten or twelve feet deep in parts, and thirty yards across . . . reserved for the sixth and fifth forms', Rugbeians spent many summer hours.[18]

In winter, especially when the ground was too hard for games, hare-and-hounds runs in the surrounding countryside would sometimes take the place of football, with ale and bread and cheese waiting at the end for those who completed the course.[19]

For boys below the Fifth Form there was always the intrusion of fagging (that is, doing menial service for senior boys); provided they could avoid this, only classes, meals, prayers, and bedtime were compulsory.[20] The rest of their time was free, but fagging could and often did occupy much of this, official when they ran messages, collected beer and food from the Buttery for the praepostors (prefects), or cleaned their shoes or studies, unofficial when they were bullied or browbeaten by the Fifth-Formers, who were not entitled to fags, to do their bidding.

Other illegal practices flourished also. Fist fights were a recognized way of settling disputes, and acceptable to the praepostors. Tom Brown's famous encounter with Slogger Williams is described at length to make the author's point that this was the proper 'English way for English boys to settle their quarrels'.[21]

Then as now, illegal drinking, too, was popular, though strongly discouraged by authority. The farewell speech of the games hero Brooke to the School House boys aptly expresses the senior boys' attitude: 'Then there's fuddling about in the public-house, and drinking bad spirits, and punch . . . that won't make good drop-kicks or chargers of you. . . . You get plenty of beer here, and that's enough for you; and drinking isn't fine or manly, whatever some of you may think of it.'[22]

Such were the main aspects of school life at Rugby during Arnold's headmastership, typical of other public schools in the early decades of the nineteenth century. What improvements did he introduce, and how successful was he in changing the boys' outlook?

3

HEADMASTER

Arnold had to be persuaded by his Oxford friends to stand for the headmastership of Rugby. Though tempted by the money, for with his expanding family he needed a larger income than that which his private school at Laleham brought him, he nevertheless had two strong reasons for hesitation.[1] First, he wanted to be sure that the Trustees of the school would not interfere with his administration. In particular, he felt strongly that expulsions should be more frequent than they were, and he feared that the Trustees' natural anxiety that the school should be full would militate against this policy. Secondly, he was unwilling to accept an appointment which he thought would involve his subscribing fully to the Thirty-Nine Articles. His decision to remain a deacon since his ordination in December 1818 had turned on this issue.[2] He was happy to agree to all the Articles that he thought fundamental to Christian belief and practice, but he had reservations, as we saw in Chapter 1, about a few that he considered unimportant, particularly the three Articles in the 36th Canon. Evidently these two objections, one practical, the other religious, must have been met, for just in time he allowed his name to go forward for the Rugby post and in June 1828, despite Dr Wooll's assurance that the Trustees would not press for it if it offended his conscience, he accepted ordination to the priesthood.

His determination to be personally free from governors' interference was matched by his belief that endowed schools should be independent of state control so that each could develop its own individuality. His view of the importance of independence, however, did not extend to the education of the middle classes; over their schools he advocated state control, in order to give them the support of a national system. By contrast, the endowed and public schools were strong enough to stand on their own.[3]

Arnold's approach to edcuation was indeed more practical than theoretical. For one who wrote so much on such a wide range of topics he wrote comparatively little on the principles of education, contenting himself in this field with a simple set of aims. The school was to be a place of Christian education in the fullest sense. Just as the idea of a Christian State seemed to him to be involved in the very idea of a State, so to him the idea of a Christian school arose naturally from the very idea of a school.[4] Its education was not simply based on religion; it was itself to be religious. Although it was his most earnest wish to introduce such a religious principle into education, writing to J. T. Coleridge the day before the start of his first term at Rugby, he expressed doubts that he would succeed.[5] He did not expect to make the boys Christian, he wrote to another friend, because of 'the natural imperfect state of boyhood', but hoped to turn out Christian men.[6] As he used to tell his praepostors, his three main aims were to inculcate, first, religious and moral principles, secondly, gentlemanly conduct, and thirdly, intellectual ability.[7] At the time this was, as indeed it would be today, a drastic reordering of priorities: duty to God and men ahead of mental training. He stressed that the way boys behaved out of school was more important to the formation of their character than what they did in class. Knowledge and love of God, reverence for law, and sympathy towards the poorer classes were more important than academic success. That Arnold's order of priority appealed to many parents is suggested by Squire Brown's reflections on what to say to Tom as he dispatched him for his first term:

I won't tell him to read his Bible, and love and serve God; if he don't do that for his mother's sake and teaching, he won't for mine. Shall I go into the sort of temptations he'll meet with? No, I can't do that. Never do for an old fellow to go into such things with a boy. He won't understand me. Do him more harm than good, ten to one. Shall I tell him to mind his work, and say he's sent to school to make himself a good scholar? Well, but he isn't sent to school for that—at any rate, not for that mainly. I don't care a straw for Greek particles, or the digamma, no more does his mother. What is he sent to school for? Well, partly because he wanted so to go. If he'll only turn out a brave, helpful, truth-telling Englishman, and a gentleman, and a Christian, that's all I want.[8]

This was a major shift of policy and, though others were thinking on similar lines and other public schools at that period had also begun to take religion and morality seriously, even if Arnold did not create the general awakening, he at least was a pioneer in action.[9] Dr Moberly, who had taught at Oxford before being appointed Head Master of Winchester, was later to testify to the immense improvement effected by Arnold on his pupils' characters,[10] and this cannot lightly be dismissed.

To achieve this improvement in the mores of a public school Arnold was convinced that boys of bad character who impeded his purpose should, without reference to the governors, be expelled. Hence his initial hesitation in applying for the Rugby post. Once the Trustees had appointed him, he expected them to let him run his own ship. He was ready to maintain friendly relations with them and glad to have their support, but he brooked no interference with either his management of the school or his engagement in public controversy on questions that were not the school's direct concern. Provided that he did not spend so much time on external politics as to make him neglect his duty to the school, and provided that he was careful not to allow his own political views to influence the boys, he was convinced that Trustees and parents had no cause to object to the expression of his views on public affairs. He felt obliged to resist any such encroachment on his position 'as a duty not only to himself but to the master of every foundation school in England'.[11] Headmasters today, regrettably, feel themselves more inhibited in this respect.

When in 1836 he was asked by an influential Trustee, Earl Howe, whether he was the author of an anonymous and savage attack in the *Edinburgh Review* entitled 'The Oxford Malignants',[12] in which he defended the liberal theologian Dr Hampden against his Tractarian critics, his reply expressed in Johnsonian style the principle which guided him:

Rugby, June 22, 1836.

My Lord,

The answer which your Lordship has asked for I have given several times to many of my friends; and I am well known to be very little apt to disavow or conceal my authorship of anything that I may at any time have written. Still as I conceive your Lordship's question to be one which none but a personal friend has the slightest right to put to me, or to any man, I feel it due to myself to decline giving an answer to it.

When Lord Howe pressed him further to comply, on the grounds that he might otherwise feel bound to take some step in case the report were true, Arnold set out his position at greater length with firmness and dignity:

June 27, 1836.

My Lord,

I am extremely sorry that you should have considered my letter as uncourteous; it was certainly not intended to be so; but I did not feel that I could answer your lordship's letter at greater length without going into greater details by way of explanation than its own shortness appeared to me to warrant. Your lordship addressed me in a tone purely formal and official, and at the same time asked a question which the common usage of society regards as one of delicacy,—justified, I do not say, only by personal friendship, but at least by some familiarity of acquaintance. It was because no such ground could exist in the present case, and because I cannot and do not acknowledge your right officially, as a Trustee of Rugby School, to question me on the subject of my real or supposed writings on matters wholly unconnected with the school, that I felt it my duty to decline answering your lordship's question.

It is very painful to be placed in a situation where I must either appear to seek concealment wholly foreign to my wishes, or else must acknowledge a right which I owe it, not only to myself, but to the master of every endowed school in England, absolutely to deny. But in the present case, I think I can hardly be suspected of seeking concealment. I have spoken on the subject of the article in the Edinburgh Review freely in the hearing of many, with no request for secrecy on their part expressed or implied. Officially, however, I cannot return an answer—not from the slightest feeling of disrespect to your lordship, but because my answering would allow a principle which I can on no account admit to be just or reasonable.[13]

The correspondence finally ended with Earl Howe moving a vote of censure at a Trustees' meeting which, if carried, might well have caused Arnold to resign. The Trustees, however, divided on the issue, four and four, and since their constitution apparently allowed no casting vote, the proposal was dropped. In writing to Dr Hawkins about this secret meeting, which Arnold got wind of only privately, he concluded his account: 'In all that passed publicly, they were all as civil as usual, and did all that I wanted about the School.'[14]

He had indeed found them civil at his first meeting with them in April 1828, four months after his appointment, and again in the following July when he had reassured them that he was not a revolutionary.[15] After the second visit he had written to tell his wife of their most encouraging disposition. They increased his salary considerably,[16] as the Report of the 1864 Clarendon Commission makes clear; some of them indeed became his friends, but others were always uneasy with him because of his Whig opinions. That in general, however, their support continued is clearly indicated by his letter to Dr Longley of 25 June 1834 ('Our little commonwealth here goes on very quietly, and I think satisfactorily. I have happily more power than Lord Grey's government, and neither Radicals to call for more, nor Tories to call for less, and so I can reform or forbear at my own discretion.'),[17] and by a resolution of the Trustees on 23 March 1836[18] issued to allay public disquiet over the March incident (discussed in Chapter 6, below):

We, the undersigned Trustees of Rugby School, assembled at an especial meeting, are glad to have an opportunity of expressing our entire satisfaction with Dr Arnold's conduct in the management of the School. Many of the young men who have proceeded to the Universities from Rugby School have distinguished themselves, and done honour to Dr Arnold's system of education, and we believe that the discipline of the School has been conducted upon most humane and liberal principles, and on this conviction we continue to repose entire confidence in Dr Arnold.[19]

It was fortunate for him that the Hampden affair was not brought before the Trustees till July of that year. A headmaster's relations with his governors are always delicate, sometimes difficult. For while he is their employee and must know that he is subject to their ultimate control in respect of the school's finances and broad policy, in the school itself day by day he is the chief authority, recognized as such by parents, masters, and boys. On his successful management the school's fortunes largely depend.

A governing body cannot itself run a school. The governors' business is to appoint the best headmaster they can find and then support him fully for as long as they have confidence in him. Once they have lost this they are entitled, indeed it is their painful duty, to cause his resignation or dismiss him. Where governors sometimes err, even today, is in lending too ready an ear to malicious gossip or overt criticism directed at their headmaster, in not trusting him enough. Headmasters lead lonely, isolated, exposed lives, and inevitably, if active, they incur criticism. This is often grossly exaggerated, for the young are naturally given to fanciful exaggeration. So headmasters need their governors' steady support, particularly when things go wrong. One main cause of the public schools' strength in the last century and a half has been the measure of independence allowed their headmasters by governing bodies and the degree of their trust in them. Arnold's stand in relation to the Rugby Trustees contributed notably to the establishment of this tradition. Today's maintained schools would be all the better if they enjoyed this benefit too.

In another important sphere headmasters of public schools have traditionally, and to their marked advantage, had greater independence of their governors than their counterparts in the maintained system—the appointment and dismissal of teaching staff. That Arnold had, at any rate towards the end of his headmastership, much of this authority is clear from the Clarendon Commissioners' Report which noted that the headmaster of Rugby usually appointed and had the power to dismiss all assistant masters except the seven senior classical masters.[20] Letters in his earlier years, however, to the Chairman of the Trustees, show that he consulted them on staff appointments which a modern headmaster would have settled himself. On 2 September 1829, for example, he asked permission to replace an inefficient teacher of French with a Monsieur Pons during the autumn without waiting until the normal Trustees' meeting the following July. Again, on 29 June 1830, he wrote: 'in compliance with what I understood to be the wishes of the Trustees, I have to recommend to them Mr Price, BA, of Worcester College, Oxford, if they should think fit to appoint him Mathematical Master to the School'. Yet a further letter from him to the Chairman, Lord Denbigh, not included in Stanley's *Life* (26 April 1831,) shows that he was aware that the Trustees regarded him as virtually responsible for the appointment of assistant staff.[21] Their approval at a Trustees' meeting was little more than a formality. So perhaps on the earlier occasions he was simply feeling his way with his new employers. He knew as well as any headmaster today the importance of the choice of teaching staff in a school. For full effectiveness a headmaster must have as his assistants those whom he can work with and through, and whom he has himself appointed. His policies are mediated through his staff and can readily be blocked, delayed, or negated by teachers unsympathetic to them. The delicate balance of elements that go to make up the chemistry of a Common Room requires subtle adjustments if the best results are to be achieved.

Soon after his appointment Arnold had written to the Trustees (29 June 1830) urging that 'nothing should be done which has a tendency to make a gentleman of independent mind feel himself lowered by accepting an assistant mastership'. From the first, he did all he could to raise his assistants' morale and status. As well as enlarging the full-time staff by three, he persuaded the Trustees to increase their salaries substantially and involved them closely in the government of the school.[22] Rarely did he act in a matter of school discipline without consulting them, and about once a month he held a masters' meeting, sometimes over dinner, to discuss school affairs in general.[23] This was an innovation which they valued highly. At these meetings he showed his confidence by encouraging considerable freedom of expression, even to the extent of allowing himself to be outvoted on an issue provided that a major principle of policy was not at stake. He was quick to give his assistants credit for their achievements and is recorded as saying of a particular master, 'nothing delights me more than to think that boys are sent here for his sake rather than mine'. In return, he had the highest expectations of them: the clerical members were no longer allowed to earn an additional salary for duties performed in nearby parishes. They might help the local clergy in the cause of good neighbourliness, but their paid service must be to the school alone. In these ways he strove to strengthen their sense of commitment and to gain their full and active co-operation as junior partners in an exciting enterprise. At the outset a few resisted the changes in established practices, but the majority not for long.

Those who did, or who otherwise failed to measure up to his high expectations he persuaded to resign or dismissed. The letter of 26 April 1831 mentioned earlier also reveals how firmly yet tactfully he handled this most unpleasant of a headmaster's duties.

My Lord,

At this moment when you must have so many other things to think of, and so soon after my former letter, it is with great reluctance that I venture to trouble your lordship again with any thing relating to the affairs of this School.—But the case is simply this, that I have for some time past felt a strong conviction that the interest of the school required Mr Moor's resignation, and having told him so, and finding him unwilling to comply with my suggestion, I have no other choice but to lay the matter before you.—In the first place however I am bound in justice to Mr Moor as well as to myself to state most expressly that there has been no personal disagreement between us, and that I have no charges of misconduct to bring against him, or of any thing to affect the high respectability of his character. But I find and have found that our views as to the state and management of the School are different, and that there is no cordial cooperation between us. This is no matter of blame to Mr Moor, and can excite no surprize; but it is a great practical inconvenience, especially as it is a fact of which the boys themselves are fully aware. At the same time, were Mr Moor's circumstances such as could make his income as master a matter of great importance to him, and had he not been so many years at the School as to make his resignation appear in itself natural and becoming, I should have been very unwilling to press for it. But as it is, since his circumstances, as I understand from his friends, are perfectly easy; and his resignation cannot seem forced or premature; I own that I feel pretty justified in calling upon him for it, that his place, important as it is, may be filled by a younger man, and one who may think and act with me more entirely and cordially.

The following order of the Trustees, made in 1747, and which I have the liberty of submitting to your lordship, leaves no doubt, I imagine, as to the question of right, although of course it does not follow that therefore it ought to be exercised. But feeling perfectly free from any personal motives, and being quite satisfied as to what the interests of the School require, I think that I should be justified in acting upon it, if Mr Moor rendered such an extreme step necessary. I have the honour to be,

My Lord,

with great respect,
Your lordship's most obedient
humble Servant,
T. Arnold.

My reason for not deferring this Matter till the Meeting of the Trustees in July, is, because some time is required to look out for a fit man to supply the vacancy, and the six weeks of the holidays would not be sufficient for that purpose.

Copy

1st August 1747. The Trustees at the same time thought it right to declare to the Assistants that they have always considered the appointment and the dismissal of any of the Assistants as virtually residing in the Head Master, whom they hold to be immediately responsible to them for the general good government of the School, and they are decidedly of opinion that it ought so to continue.

What qualities he looked for in new recruits to his staff are best described in his own words, in two letters preserved in Stanley's biography. The first sets out his requirements for a lower classical form master who might yet have some teaching higher up the school, in the Fifth or Sixth:

What I want is a man who is a Christian and a gentleman, an active man, and one who has common sense, and understands boys. I do not so much care about scholarship, as he will have immediately under him the lowest forms in the school; but yet, on second thoughts, I do care about it very much, because his pupils may be in the highest forms; and besides, I think that even the elements are best taught by a man who has a thorough knowledge of the matter. However, if one must give way, I prefer activity of mind and an interest in his work to high scholarship: for the one may be acquired far more easily than the other. I should wish it also to be understood, that the new master may be called upon to take boarders in his house, it being my intention for the future to require this of all masters as I see occasion, that so in time the boarding-houses may die a natural death. . . . With this to offer, I think I have a right to look rather high for the man whom I fix upon, and it is my great object to get here a society of intelligent, gentlemanly, and active men, who may permanently keep up the character of the school, and make it '*vile damnum*' if I were to break my neck tomorrow.

The second letter sets out his ideal to a master on his appointment:

The qualifications which I deem essential to the due performance of a master's duties here, may in brief be expressed as the spirit of a Christian and a gentleman,—that a man should enter upon his business not ἐκ παρέργου, but as a substantive and most important duty; that he should devote himself to it as the especial branch of the ministerial calling which he has chosen to follow—that belonging to a great public institution, and standing in a public and conspicuous situation, he should study things 'lovely and of good report'; that is, that he should be public spirited, liberal, and entering heartily into the interest, honour, and general respectability and distinction of the society which he has joined; and that he should have sufficient vigour of mind and thirst for knowledge, to persist in adding to his own stores without neglecting the full improvement of those whom he is teaching. I think our masterships here offer a noble field of duty, and I would not bestow them on any one whom [*sic*] I thought would undertake them without entering into the spirit of our system heart and hand.[24]

Just as he himself took pains to keep his brain active by his writing and scholarship, so he expected his staff to do likewise.[25] Regrettably few today, whether headmasters or assistants, manage to find time for both original academic work and the claims of a full teaching programme. The success of Arnold's recruitment policy and subsequent management of staff is shown by the devotion he inspired in them and by the later careers of men like Bonamy Price, who was elected Professor of Political Economy at Oxford, and J. Prince Lee, G. G. Bradley, and H. Hill, who became headmasters and influenced their schools in ways significantly different from

Arnold. Two fine expressions of this devotion can be found in Prince Lee's letter of resignation written in the term before he took over King Edward's School, Birmingham, and in an extract from the diary of the Revd Algernon Grenfell, a member of the Rugby staff at the time of Arnold's death:

Rugby, Warwickshire, June 19, 1838.

My Dear Dr Arnold,

I have written my letter of resignation to Lord Denbigh. There remains for me one other duty before I close my connection with Rugby School.

It is to return you my most grateful thanks for all that, under God, you for the last eight years have done for me and mine. For your invariable kindness, courtesy, and liberality, for the information and advice I have gained from you, and the advancement and support you extended to me in the School I, from my heart, most sincerely thank you. But for what I feel especially I have derived from you, a knowledge of higher aims and a desire to aim at a simpler, truer course of life and thought, I cannot thank you merely as for an advantage gained, for I feel at the same time at once the privilege it gives and the responsibility which it entails on me. But it is your best thanks that you have my assurance of my humble hope and wish, that what you have taught I may be able to persist in, and that though distant, we may still be fellow-labourers till at last we meet for ever.

Forgive my troubling you with these expressions of my feeling. You do not want them, but it is a relief and pleasure to me to give vent to them. I shall indeed be sorry if you do not allow me any opportunity to show my sense of what I owe you by any service to you or your children. That God may bless you, dear Mrs Arnold, and them, is the earnest wish both of myself and of my wife.

Believe me ever with sincerest esteem and respect,

Your deeply obliged and affectionate friend,
James Prince Lee[26]

The Revd Algernon Grenfell's diary entry for Sunday, 12 June 1842 reads:

While dressing this morning I received the message from the School House of the death of my dear and most *valued friend and father*, Dr Arnold. . . . So fled to the bosom of its God, to the presence of its Saviour the spirit of one of God's most faithful Servants, of Christ's truest disciples—So has the Church of God lost one of her pillars, one of her brightest and finest lights.

So has England lost one of her wisest and best and greatest men.

So have all who knew and loved, and were loved by his great spirit lost a friend and a father in Israel.[27]

How few headmasters, even if they were to die in office, would today arouse such sentiments. These were, however, at least in part, due to the special position that Arnold took in the school community by being chaplain as well as headmaster.[28] That he regarded this dual role as centrally important is clear from his letter to the Trustees in 1831 asking them to appoint him to the chaplaincy which had just fallen vacant with the resignation of the Revd C. A. Anstey. It seemed to him 'the natural and fitting thing . . . that the master of the boys should be officially as well as really their pastor, and that he should not devolve on another, however well qualified, one of his most peculiar and solemn duties'. From the autumn of that year, the Trustees having granted his request, insisting that he draw the chaplain's salary which he had offered to forgo,[29] he preached in chapel almost every Sunday of the school year for the rest of his life.[30]

The combination of headmaster and chaplain was not new. In the centuries when most scholars were in holy orders, governing bodies of schools naturally looked among those in holy orders when electing a headmaster, and it was not until well into the twentieth century that clerical headmasters ceased to be the norm. Now they are the exception, and a dog-collar is regarded by many governing bodies as a handicap. Certainly the range of choice would be undesirably narrowed if the old custom still prevailed. But most governing bodies of public schools still expect their headmasters to be communicant members of the Church of England or of Churches in communion therewith, so the relevance of Christian faith and practice to the administration of the school continues to be recognized. That this should be so in this irreligious age is a tribute to Arnold and other nineteenth-century headmasters whose use of their special position as priests had so powerful an effect on succeeding generations of their pupils. Though there are now far fewer chapel services and though modern headmasters preach far less, rarely more than once or twice a term, most of them still regard the influence of the chapel and what takes place there as profoundly important.[31] Indeed one of the particular characteristics of the public school today continues to be its emphasis on the importance of the pupils' religious upbringing. Godliness, though no longer expressed in such language, nor so strongly or as effectively as in Arnold's day, is still actively promoted.

Another, not dissimilar, reduction in a headmaster's pastoral effectiveness has also occurred this century. Very few, if any, headmasters are today housemasters as well. Yet it was probably among the boys of the School House, the main boarding-house over which he presided, that Arnold's influence was most strongly felt. Apart from those in the Sixth Form whom Arnold taught, they would have been closest to him. Though feared and disliked at the start of his time, because of his desire to reform the ways of the school, by 1839 he had won the School House boys' loyalty.[32] When he announced in that year that he intended to resign housemastering as a first step towards retiring altogether at the end of 1842, he was earnestly requested to change his mind. 'Sir', wrote H. Doxat, Head of House, 'We, the undersigned, have heard with regret your intention of giving up the School House. We venture to say that the personal regard we feel for you would make us extremely lament your leaving us; and we humbly hope that this expression of our feelings may be allowed some weight in influencing your determination.'[33]

The petition, signed also by sixty-three others including Thomas Hughes, changed Arnold's mind. Yet though this appeal and the testimony of former pupils make clear the boys' respect for him, the picture of life in School House that emerges from the pages of *Tom Brown's Schooldays*, which Hughes's contemporaries considered fair and accurate so far as it goes and which covers the central years of Arnold's headmastership, does not suggest that his housemasterly influence had fundamentally affected conditions there. When there were responsible boys at the top, life for their juniors was tolerable; when authority was in the hands of big boys not yet fit for a share in government or of small young boys who had reached the top through cleverness, then 'all threatened to return into darkness and chaos again', with the tyrant Flashman unrestrained, the house divided into rival cliques, and other signs of disorder such as excessive beer drinking, and brutal bullying of boys. Arnold in fact seems to have been the type of housemaster who interferes little in the running of the boys' side. He was usually present in the hall for call over at dinner and always, unless prevented, took House Prayers every evening at 9.45 p.m., and through what his praepostors chose to tell him he knew much of what went on, but he rarely visited the boys' side unless he had wind of trouble, such as a noise or disturbance in the dormitories or a fight in the hall on a wet day.[34] On one occasion recorded by Hughes, when he wanted to call on a particular boy, he had to ask the way to his study. It may surprise the modern observer that in so small a school as Rugby was then he was not a more visible presence, but it must be remembered that in housemasters at that period such aloofness was the norm, and he himself did not enjoy being a housemaster. He found it wearisome, indeed, as he grew older, the most irksome part of his work.[35]

Arnold was indeed shy and awkward with adolescents. The very young, under 13, he knew how to handle, treating them like children, sympathizing with their animal spirits and playing with them, or going over their work with them on his knee. With the Sixth Forms, too, who at 17 and 18 were almost men, he had close and good relations. The library, where he taught them day by day, was, except for the chapel, the sphere of his greatest influence. But despite his youthful temperament he had little sympathy with the boys in the middle of the school. Boyish misbehaviour he treated as sinful. Naughtiness to him was wickedness, schools were nurseries of vice. He seems to have forgotten how leniently he had expected his headmaster at Winchester to deal with him when as a prefect he was caught playing cards illegally for money. He could not appreciate boys' moral thoughtlessness and natural levity about what to him were important matters. 'A great school is very trying,' he wrote, 'so much of sin combined with so little of sorrow.' 'With boys of the richer classes, one sees nothing but plenty, health, and youth; and these are really awful to behold when one must feel they are unblessed.' Part of the gaiety of youth, he said, is like the gaiety of a drunken man, riotous, indolent, and annoying to others, and he had no sympathy with boyhood as a natural stage in growing up. Though he saw the dangers in his attitude, he was ever looking for boys to be responsible and adult before their time.[36] 'Can the change from childhood to manhood be hastened,' he asked, 'without prematurely exhausting the faculties of body and mind?'[37] The absence of suspicion, the instinctive courtesy, the openness with which he treated all boys were not enough to dispel their natural distrust of authority, especially when it demanded such high standards so uncompromisingly. Since a later chapter will discuss more fully the methods of punishment by which he sought to regulate the boys' behaviour, it is enough to say here that these were bound to reinforce the awe and fear in which he was held by them. Not until his last years, when he had learnt to tolerate a low standard of morality among the boys, did his moral transparency and his consistency of behaviour and outlook evoke from most of them affection, loyalty, and esteem.

Older boys, however, were earlier much more susceptible to his influence.[38] Stanley's picture of Arnold's relations with former pupils may be somewhat idealized, for he *par excellence* benefited from close friendship with his former headmaster, but its main features are confirmed by the experience of others who were on less intimate terms. Members of the Sixth Form were invited to Fox How in the holidays to refresh their health, for Arnold believed that mountains and dales were 'a great point in education',[39] besides which he could get to know them better away from school surroundings. After his first four years at Rugby there were often old boys visiting School House during term time, glad to renew a relationship that had influenced them so strongly when they were still at school. With many of them he corresponded at length, some he helped prepare for university examinations or advised on careers,[40] to others he gave books or even money. On visits to Oxford, where most of his boys had been sent (404 in all, compared with 223 to Cambridge),[41] he saw great numbers of them and was well received. As he wrote on 7 October 1835, 'my intercourse with my old pupils . . . is to me one of the freshest springs of my life'.[42]

At the start of his time at Rugby he had not endeared himself to any of his pupils, young or old. For, as Hughes described him, he was thought 'somewhat of a fanatic in matters of change'. As he explained later to Stanley, 'My love for any place or person, or institution, is exactly the measure of my desire to reform them.'[43] But boys are arch-conservatives and do not welcome reformers, while assistant masters are more often than not set in their ways and dislike changes of routine. So he soon found that the task of reforming Rugby was much harder than he had expected.[44] But gradually all came to realize that he did not make changes for the sake of change and that behind them were strongly held principles that gave his reforms coherence.[45] While he altered many of the old customs, he did not meddle with those he thought worth keeping and most of his changes were slight shifts in emphasis, the quiet replacement of bad with good, the adaptation of traditional practices to new and worthwhile ends.[46] Even the reform for which he has been given most credit, the prefectorial system, which will be considered in a later chapter, was not as large as has often been thought. His main achievement was not so much any one reform as a general improvement of atmosphere which resulted from many slight adjustments.[47]

One particular development for which he has often been blamed, the growth of athleticism in public schools, the subordination of academic work to organized games, he had no hand in. Nor did his natural sympathies lie in that direction. Aristotelian as he was, he would have agreed with that philosopher's denunciation of the intense gymnastic training which brutalized the Spartan young.[48] At Winchester as a boy he showed no particular talent for, or attraction to, organized school games. He was happiest attacking or defending an imaginary fort on the downs. At Rugby he neither refers to, nor draws lessons from, games in his sermons, letters, journals, or educational writings. At no time did he think or suggest that games formed any part of an assistant master's responsibilities.[49] His son Thomas said that his father was no sportsman. By modern standards indeed he could more reasonably be blamed for lack of enthusiasm for organized games. Thomas Hughes, for example, described his departure to his Lakeland holiday home the day before the cricket 1st XI were due to play two important end-of-term matches. He did no more before he left than see the captain of the XI to discuss the arrangments for entertaining the visiting teams and to lay down a few rules to ensure good behaviour by the boys. In fact he was nothing like as assiduous in supporting his house or the school on the touchline or boundary as most headmasters today. He would sometimes stand in his garden above the wall and watch the boys playing football,[50] and it was a matter for comment if he came on to the Close to watch a team for as long as half an hour, as Peter Brooke's farewell speech to School House shows: 'If I saw him stopping football, or cricket, or bathing, or sparring, I'd be as ready as any fellow to stand up about it. But he don't—he encourages them; didn't you see him out today for half an hour watching us? (Loud cheers for the Doctor.)'[51]

Arnold's encouragement was to enjoy physical exercise of any type just as he did—country walks, bathing, running, and leaping about, not organized games in particular. The myth of Arnold's athleticism was largely the creation of the widely read *Tom Brown's Schooldays*, whose author, being a spirited schoolboy without academic inclinations, omitted almost entirely the intellectual side of school life and Arnold's promotion of it. An earlier extract from Brooke's speech, 'I'd sooner win two School House matches running than get the Balliol Scholarship any day', which received frantic cheers, points the difference.[52]

All worthwhile extra-curricular activities won Arnold's support, not one more than another. When the boys started a school magazine he felt 'unmixed pleasure in its going on', provided it was not political or contentious. 'I delight in the spirit of it,' was his comment in October 1835, 'and think there is much ability in many of the articles. I think also that it is likely to do good to the school.'[53] He similarly approved of the establishment of societies for debating[54] and drama. He and his wife attended performances and were as enthusiastic as the boys in their acclaim. When Samuel Sandes acted with such sincerity his part in Sheridan's *The Rivals* that he wept, Arnold showed his appreciation by inviting the boy to breakfast with his family the next day.[55]

Mrs Arnold's role as headmaster's wife is all too easily overlooked, as often happens also with many headmasters today. Too often their wives' contribution to a school's well-being, through cherishing their husband, which is their most valuable task, is ignored or inadequately appreciated by outside observers. Stanley's biography, probably at her own insistence, barely mentions her, but his letters are testimony to her courage, decisiveness, and wise counsel, and it is clear from the later correspondence of former pupils how significant were her support for her husband, her restraint of his natural impetuosity, and her influence in School House. Her afternoon ride with him walking beside her, already noted in the first chapter, doubtless gave them both a welcome opportunity to discuss school as well as family problems, and passages in *Tom Brown's Schooldays*, dedicated to her without her permission, show that, in addition to providing a happy family background in School House, she actively promoted her husband's plans. When Tom, who had returned to school at the start of a new half-year hoping to share a double study with East, his close friend and cheerful accomplice in 'illegal' escapades, is instead asked to share with a delicate, nervous, thirteen-year-old new boy, George Arthur, it is Mrs Arnold's authority that the matron relies on to overcome his reluctance.[56] And it is Mrs Arnold's invitation to Tom and George to have tea with her that same day that clinches the arrangement. Thomas Hughes indeed uses this tea-party to pay his own tribute to her, pointing out how many Old Rugbeians looked back with fond and grateful memories to that School House drawing-room, and dated much of their highest and best training to the lessons learnt there.[57] Such memories were not confined to boys in School House. Stanley, who was in Mr Anstey's House, remembered her visiting him in the sick-room.[58] Albert Pell, later Member of Parliament for South Leicestershire, recalled her kindness to him after his father's death.[59] More striking still is the tribute paid her by her fourth son, William, in a letter to greet her on her birthday at Fox How in August 1842. Back at Rugby at the start of the new school year, after talking about his father's recent death and his own efforts in school, he wrote, 'Oh my darling, how everybody does love you.'[60]

One out-of-school activity, community service, promoted by public schools in the last twenty-five years, Arnold advocated in his sermons, but there is no evidence that Rugbeians of his day, despite their headmaster's personal example, took his imaginative advice to heart, and put it into practice.

> A young man of an active and powerful mind, advancing rapidly in knowledge . . . should go . . . to the abodes of poverty and sickness and old age. Everything there is a lesson. . . . Accustomed to all the comforts of life . . . he sees poverty and all its evils—scanty room, and too often scanty fuel, scanty clothing, and scanty food. Instead of the quiet and neatness of his own chamber, he finds very often, a noise and a confusion which would render deep thought impossible. . . . Nor is this most profitable duty of visiting the poor . . . one which you can only practise hereafter, and which does not concern you here. . . . It would indeed . . . make this place really a seminary of true religion and useful learning if those among us who are of more thoughtful years . . . could remember that he cannot learn in Christ's school who does not acquaint himself something with the poor.[61]

From first to last his letters show how much, despite its inevitable trials, he enjoyed headmastering. In October 1831 he described Rugby as 'the scene of wholesome and happy labour, offering as much to refresh the inward man, with as little to disturb him as this earth, since Paradise, . . . could ever present to any one individual'.[62] On another occasion he wrote: 'If ever I could receive a new boy from his father without emotion, I should think it was high time to be off.'[63] Indeed at one time he thought that he would not stay longer than about fifteen years.[64] He found the work engrossing, with never enough time for all that needed to be done.[65] When Mr Justice Coleridge criticized him for spending too much time writing on public affairs and matters of general interest not connected with the school, he was quick to defend himself. His writing on public affairs, mostly done in the holidays, did not distract him from his prime duty to the school. Rather, it refreshed him. Spared much of a modern headmaster's routine—conferences away from school, educational committees in London and elsewhere, dealing with the media—he considered that Rugby was no burden, but 'the thing of all others which I believe to be most fitted for me while I am well and in the vigour of life' (letter to Chevalier Bunsen, 13 June 1840).[66]

The end came sooner than he or anyone except for Mrs Arnold expected. Her diary suggests that she had some premonition. His fourteenth year at the school was drawing to its close; on 5 June he had preached his farewell sermon in chapel, and this had been followed by the usual crush of business at the end of a long half-year—examination of the Fifth Form, the year's visits by the Oxford and Cambridge examiners and by former pupils going down for the vacation, the school speech day on Friday, 10 June. At nine o'clock on the Saturday evening, with the boys due to disperse the following day, he entertained the School House Sixth-Formers to supper and was at his most cheerful and lively. The entry for that night in his diary, which he had started in May, perhaps suggests that he had some inkling of what was to come. 'Saturday Evening, June 11th. The day after tomorrow will be my birthday, if I am permitted to live to see it.—My forty-seventh birthday since my birth; how large a portion of that life which I am to pass upon earth. And then? What is to follow this life? How visibly my outward work in this world seems contracting and softening away into the gentler employments of old age. In one sense how nearly can I say, *Vixi*. And I thank God that as far as ambition is concerned, it is I trust mortified fully: I have no desire other than to step back gradually from my present place in the world, and not to rise to an higher one. But yet there are works which I would do with God's permission, before the night cometh—And that great work, if I might be permitted to take a part in it. But let me above all mind my own personal work, to keep myself pure and zealous and believing, labouring to do God's will, but not anxious that it should be done by me rather than by others, if God disapproves of my doing it.'[67]

Between 5 a.m. and 6 a.m. on the Sunday morning he was woken by a sharp chest pain, which his wife feared was angina pectoris. As the pain increased and his manner seemed unusually earnest, especially as he quoted verses from the New Testament, she sent for their doctor. When his son Tom came in to see him, he said, 'My son, thank God for me. Thank God for having sent me this pain. I never had pain before, and I feel it is good for me, and I am *so* thankful.' On being told that he was suffering from spasm of the heart, and asked by the doctor whether any of his family had a similar disease, he evidently realized that his end was near. His father had died of it at 53. 'Is it suddenly fatal?' he asked. 'Yes, suddenly fatal.' After many further questions about the disease, 'Is it generally fatal?' 'Yes, I am afraid it is.' Shortly before 8 a.m., after Mary Arnold had read a passage from the prayer book's Order for the Visitation of the Sick and after further spasms of acute pain, he died.[68]

The following Friday, 17 June, he was buried at 11 a.m. under the communion table in the chapel, where he had so often preached. On 22 June the Arnold family set off by rail to Fox How. As the Revd Algernon Grenfell, one of the pallbearers at the funeral, wrote in his diary: 'In the early morning of June 12th Dr Arnold was in health and strength. In the morning of June 22nd all that were his had left Rugby and he had himself lain five days in the silent grave.'[69]

4

PREACHING

To regular preaching in chapel and to the services held there Arnold attached great importance. Hence his wish to be chaplain as well as headmaster. Though separate treatment of his pastoral from his headmagisterial role is artifical, for the two were, in Arnold's mind, inextricably united, it is a distinct aspect of his work that is worth consideration on its own.

Unquestionably the school chapel was central to his activities. A small building by comparison with chapels built later at other major public schools, 90 feet long by 30 feet wide, it was the first chapel of any size to be built for a school other than Winchester and Eton. Neo-Gothic in style, of white brick dressed in Attleborough stone, with pews facing inwards and an ante-chapel at the west end, it was, except for its pulpit and flat ceiling, very similar in size and appearance to the present chapel of Corpus Christi College, Cambridge, completed in 1827 and likewise designed for corporate worship rather than private devotions. It had been consecrated, and dedicated to St Laurence, as recently as 1820, the last of Dr Wooll's buildings, much needed before this because the gallery in the parish church, set aside for the boys, had for many years provided seats for fewer than half of the school, so that Big School had to be used for the overflow. The new building, however, was large enough to seat only some 300 boys and, with further expansion of the school's numbers after Arnold's time, had later to be replaced, as we saw in Chapter 2. Thus little is now left of the chapel of his day, the chief remains being the altar, somewhat enlarged, some masters' stalls, the pulpit, and the east window depicting the Adoration of the Magi.

This window, containing some fine stained glass from Louvain, the gift of the masters, was one of five that were fitted during his headmastership as part of his policy of giving the new chapel as much character as possible. To the same end he had a vault built beneath it to hold the bodies of those who died at the school. Appropriately enough, his was the first to be buried there, the only headmaster to this day to lie within the chapel walls, immortalized by the poem, 'Rugby Chapel', of his agnostic eldest son, Matthew.[1]

Coldly, sadly descends
The autumn-evening. The field
Strewn with its dark yellow drifts
Of wither'd leaves, and the elms,
Fade into dimness apace,
Silent;—hardly a shout
From a few boys late at their play!
The lights come out in the street,
In the schoolroom windows—but cold,
Solemn, unlighted, austere,
Through the gathering darkness, arise
The chapel-walls, in whose bound
Thou, my father! art laid.

There thou dost lie, in the gloom
Of the autumn evening. But ah!
That word, *gloom*, to my mind
Brings thee back in the light
Of thy radiant vigour again;
In the gloom of November we pass'd
Days not dark by thy side;
Seasons impair'd not the ray
Of thine even cheerfulness clear.
Such thou wast! and I stand
In the autumn evening and think
Of bygone autumns with thee.

. . .

Yes, in some far-shining sphere,
Conscious or not of the past,
Still thou performest the word
Of the Spirit in whom thou dost live—
Prompt, unwearied, as here!
Still thou upraisest with zeal
The humble good from the ground,
Sternly repressest the bad.
Still, like a trumpet, dost rouse
Those who with half-open eyes
Tread the border-land dim
'Twixt vice and virtue; reviv'st,
Succourest!—this was thy work,
This was thy life upon earth.

What effect Matthew's father's sermons had on the boys is still more powerfully described by Thomas Hughes:

The oak pulpit standing out by itself above the School seats. The tall gallant form, the kindling eye, the voice, now soft as the low notes of a flute, now clear and stirring as the call of the light infantry bugle, of him who stood there Sunday after Sunday, witnessing and pleading for his Lord, the King of righteousness and love and glory, with whose spirit he was filled, and in whose power he spoke. The long lines of young faces, rising tier above tier down the whole length of the chapel, from the little boy's who had just left his mother to the young man's who was going out next week into the great world rejoicing in his strength . . .

But what was it after all which seized and held these three hundred boys, dragging them out of themselves, willing or unwilling, for twenty minutes, on Sunday afternoons? True, there always were boys scattered up and down the School, who in heart and head were worthy to hear and able to carry away the deepest and wisest words there spoken. But these were a minority always, generally a very small one. . . . What was it that moved and held us, the rest of the three hundred reckless childish boys, who feared the Doctor with all our hearts, and very little besides in heaven or earth: who thought more of our sets in the School than of the Church of Christ, and put the traditions of Rugby and the public opinion of boys in our daily life above the laws of God? We couldn't enter into half that we heard; we hadn't the knowledge of our own hearts or the knowledge of one another; and little enough of the faith, hope, and love needed to that end. But we listened, as all boys in their better moods will listen . . . to a man who [*sic*] we felt to be, with all his heart and soul and strength, striving against whatever was mean and unmanly and unrighteous in our little world. It was not the cold clear voice of one giving advice and warning from serene heights to those who were struggling and sinning below, but the warm living voice of one who was fighting for us and by our sides, and calling on us to help him and ourselves and one another. And so, wearily and little by little, but surely and steadily on the whole, was brought home to the young boy, for the first time, the meaning of his life: that it was no fool's or sluggard's paradise into which he had wandered by chance, but a battle-field ordained from of old, where there are no spectators, but the youngest must take his side, and the stakes are life and death.[2]

That the author of *Tom Brown's Schooldays* should have been so affected surprised Stanley, who saw small resemblance in Hughes's picture of Rugby to the school that he had known.[3] Stanley himself of course, as might be expected of a boy who was later to be a Dean, revelled in the sermons. He and his friend Charles Vaughan, the future Head Master of Harrow, 'used to nudge each other with delight'[4] as Arnold mounted the pulpit steps, and after the service Stanley would hurry back to his study to write down all that he had heard. His enthusiasm was doubtless exceptional, but others are on record as being profoundly moved by his sermons.

Stanley records the words of one who, while admitting that the sermons had little practical effect on him, was nevertheless much moved by them at the time: 'I used to listen to them from first to last with a kind of awe, and over and over again could not join my friends at the Chapel door, but would walk home to be alone; and I remember the same effects being produced by them, more or less, on others, whom I should have thought as hard as stones, and on whom I should think Arnold looked as some of the worst boys in the school.'[5]

What was it that stirred the hearts of such different boys so strongly? A schoolboy congregation is easily bored and, when boys face each other across the aisle, can quickly become restless. Evensong at four o'clock in the afternoon was hardly a time or an occasion conducive to concentration. Arnold's voice was not particularly musical nor were his words especially eloquent. He was indeed criticized for the baldness of his language, his *ex cathedra* tone, the hardness and severity, and the excessive demands that he made on his pupils. He himself agreed with a critic that he had not adequately represented the Gospel's intense mercy but argued that this was the consequence of his labouring to express its purity. His abhorrence of the evil that he thought he saw in a public school distorted his judgement, as is well illustrated in his sermon on Galatians 3:24:

What the aspect of public schools is, when viewed with a Christian's eye,—and what are the feelings with which men, who do really turn to God in after life, look back upon their years passed at school,—I cannot express better than in the words of one who had himself been at a public school, who did afterwards become a most exemplary Christian, and who, in what I am going to quote, seems to describe his own experience: 'Public schools,' he says, 'are the very seats and nurseries of vice. It may be unavoidable, or it may not; but the fact is indisputable. None can pass through a large school without being pretty intimately acquainted with vice; and few, alas! very few, without tasting too largely of that poisoned bowl. The hour of grace and repentance at length arrives, and they are astonished at their former fatuity. The young convert looks back with inexpressible regret to those hours which have been wasted in folly, or worse than folly: and the more lively his sense of the newly discovered mercies, the more piercing his anguish for past indulgences.' Now, although too many of us may not be able to join in the last part of this description, yet we must all, I think, be able to bear witness to the truth of the first part. We may not all share in the after repentance, but we must know that our school life has given ample cause for repentance.

But, it may be asked, what is meant when public schools are called 'the seats and nurseries of vice?' It is not difficult to find out in what sense a Christian writer must have used the expression. That is properly a nursery of vice, where a boy unlearns the pure and honest principles which he may have received at home, and gets, in their stead, others which are utterly low, and base, and mischievous,—where he loses his modesty, his respect for truth, and his affectionateness, and becomes coarse, and false, and unfeeling. That, too, is a nursery of vice, and most fearfully so, where vice is bold, and forward, and presuming; and goodness is timid and shy, and existing as if by sufferance,—where the good, instead of setting the tone of society, and branding with disgrace those who disregard it, are themselves exposed to reproach for their goodness, and shrink before the open avowal of evil principles, which the bad are striving to make the law of the community. That is a nursery of vice, where the restraints laid upon evil are considered as so much taken from liberty, and where, generally speaking, evil is more willingly screened and concealed, than detected and punished. What society would be, if men regarded the laws of God and man as a grievance, and thought liberty consisted in following to the full their proud, and selfish, and low inclinations,—that schools to a great extent are: and, therefore, they may be well called 'the seats and nurseries of vice.'[6]

This is extreme stuff, yet such fervour of delivery, such earnest seriousness of language, plain and unadorned by literary device, got through to all but the youngest of his audience. He made no attempt to hide his emotions, even on occasions breaking into tears when he spoke of the agonies of the crucifixion. Only the members of the Sixth Form probably grasped to the full the originality of his ideas, but all could see that he was not talking down to them, and could appreciate the sincerity, simplicity, and burning conviction with which these ideas were advanced. Written, moreover, as his eldest daughter describes, between the morning and afternoon services of the same day, his sermons were short, forceful, and direct, with a practicality and intimacy that appealed to many in the congregation. He seldom preached for more than twenty minutes, and always, as he said, 'in the language of common life and applied to the cases of common life'.[7] He talked of common faults which boys committed every day, common feelings which every day passed through their hearts and minds. While only rarely touching on sexual misbehaviour, he roundly condemned unbelief and uncharitableness, drunkenness, incurring debts, wasting money or time, immoderate intellectual and physical exercise, and neglect of duty.[8] Such a break from conventional pulpit themes and jargon and from technical theological language, and such brevity, set the pattern for the school sermon of today.

An extract from a sermon delivered early in his time at Rugby provides an apt illustration:

Several of you are only just come to this place; some of you were never at any school at all till you came here. Some of you, at least, and I hope very many, have had the blessing of good parents at home; you have been taught to hear of God, and of Christ, to say your prayers, and to remember that wherever you are, and whatever you are doing, God ever sees you. You have seen in your own house nothing base, nothing cruel, nothing ill-natured, and especially, nothing false. You thought a lie was one of the most hateful things in the world; and that to give up to your brothers and sisters, and to please your parents, was a great deal better than to be always quarrelling and envying, and to think of pleasing no one but yourselves. I hope and believe that many of you, before you came to school, were thus taught, and that the teaching was not in vain; that you not only heard of what was good, but, on the whole, practised it.

But how is it with you now? I am afraid that I dare not ask those who have been here so much as one half year or more: but even if I were to ask those who have not yet been here so much as one month, what sort of an answer could you give, if you answered truly? Do you think of God *now*? Do you remember that He ever, and in every place, sees what you are doing? Do you say your prayers to Him? Do you still think that lying, and all those shuffling, dishonest excuses, which are as bad as lying, are base, and contemptible, and wicked?—or have you heard these things so often from others, even if you yourselves have not been guilty of them, that you think there cannot be any great harm in them? Do you still love to be kind to your companions, never teasing or ill-treating them, and never being ill-natured and out of temper with them?—or have you already been accustomed to the devilish pleasure of giving pain to others: and whilst you are yourselves teased and ill-used by some who are stronger than you, do you repeat the very same conduct to those who are weaker than you? Are you still anxious to please your parents; and, in saying your lessons, do you still retain the natural thought of a well-bred and noble disposition, that you would like to say them as well as you can, and to please those who teach you?—or have you already learnt the first lesson in the devil's school, to laugh at what is good, and generous, and high-principled, and to be ashamed of doing your duty?[9]

That there was too much insistence, especially in the earlier sermons, on sin, judgement, punishment, and eternal torment cannot be gainsaid. He justified his constant efforts to convince his pupils of their guilt by his desire to save them from damnation and by his awareness of their deafness to his appeal. To his friend the Revd George Cornish he wrote in August 1830: '. . . it is quite awful to watch the strength of evil in such young minds, and how powerless is every effort against it. It would give the vainest man alive a very fair notion of his own insufficiency, to see how little he can do, and how his most earnest addresses are as a cannonball on a bolster; thorough careless unimpressibleness beats me all to pieces.'[10]

While he doubtless did not know that copies of the prayer book, specially written by one of his assistant masters for the boys' use, were often kicked up and down the House corridors in lieu of a football, he would have been aware of their response to his appeal for chapel funds—orders for £1,000 upon the 'Bank of Elegance' and innumerable buttons.[11] Most Rugbians were no more or less religious than boys of any time or place. Boys could not kneel in the dormitories for prayer without being mocked or assailed by flying boots. As one of his former pupils put it, 'if the devil had flown away with [the chapel], it would have been a matter of no concern to me'.

Yet to those boys who listened to his sermons, their chief novelty and excellence were the practical advice on behaviour, the good sense expressed in the language of reality, more often than not accompanied by some expression of encouragement.[12] The love of home and of truth, the conditions of honest intellectual work, the responsibility of the talented to share their gifts in service to others—these were his most common themes, but he varied them from time to time with sermons on the interpretation of the Bible or on the general principles of Christianity or arguments for it.[13] Above all he dealt continuously with the character and example of Christ, drawing out the implications of Christian faith for everyday attitudes and behaviour. Yet he was almost always careful to avoid controversial issues whether in politics or in theology, for he aimed not so much to persuade his boys to take a particular point of view on different matters as to develop their moral idealism in general.[14] The individual's independence of mind he respected and encouraged as long as his moral foundations were firm. But for some the moral pressure was too intense, so that, as with the poet A. H. Clough, their foundations crumbled when they were no longer under Arnold's spell and they lost their faith and sense of direction.

Edward Balston, Head Master of Eton, expressed this criticism to the Clarendon Commissioners when they questioned why he did not himself preach:

I think that the religious character formed by it [Dr Arnold's preaching] was not so genuine as it should have been. Boys are so easily influenced and so easily impressed with anything which is said from the pulpit, that it requires great consideration whether the man who is placed over them as Head Master should be the man who should influence them so extensively as I consider the Head Master would have the power of doing if he had the right of preaching to them. I think it would rather tend to destroy the purity and freedom, and therefore the thorough simplicity of their religion.[15]

With the passing of the years Arnold's tone of preaching became less severe. As he came to know his pupils and how best to convey his message, he made more use of exhortation and less of denunciation, appealing to the boys' better nature rather than censuring their faults. In particular, his sermons to leavers at their point of departure for Oxford and Cambridge struck them as specially full of feeling and good advice, and made some for the first time realize how much he cared for them.[16]

The real point which concerns us all is not whether our sin be of one kind or another, more or less venial, or more or less mischievous in man's judgement, and to our wordly interests; but whether we struggle against all sin because it is sin; whether we have or have not placed ourselves consciously under the banner of our Lord Jesus Christ, trusting in Him, cleaving to Him, feeding on Him by faith daily, and so resolved, and continually renewing our resolution, to be His faithful soldiers and servants to our lives' end. To this I would call you all, so long as I am permitted to speak to you—to this I do call you all and especially all who are likely to meet here again after a short interval, that you may return Christ's servants with a believing and loving heart; and, if this be so, I care little as to what particular form temptations from without may take; there will be a security within—a security not of man, but of God.[17]

Although, despite his dominant desire to make the school a Christian community and the chapel the centre of the school's religious life, he did not introduce a daily service there and masters continued to take prayers in Big School each morning in rotation,[18] he did introduce lectures on Sunday mornings and afternoons and the use of a short prayer in the Sixth Form at the start of the day's work.[19] Prayers were also said in each boarding-house at night.[20] This last practice, widespread in public schools since Arnold's time, has only in the last twenty years or so begun to die out or be replaced by secular evening meetings of boys in a house.

The popularity of his sermons was not the only improvement he effected in chapel worship. He and the boarding housemasters took great trouble over the preparation of boys for confirmation, and he arranged for the confirmation service to be held in chapel every other year; it is now normal practice for public schools to hold this service at least once, if not twice, a year. He expected those who had been confirmed at school to take their first communion there rather than at home.[21] He also encouraged boys below the Sixth Form to attend communion, and at the four services each year he persuaded, on a few occasions by a special appeal, as many as 100 to attend. The usual number was about 70. Once the entire Sixth Form stayed to take communion, and he was much moved and delighted,[22] for he saw the service as being concerned not only with God but also with one's fellows, so that the good feelings of genuine companionship it generated counterbalanced the evil combinations of boys that he thought so harmful to the school.[23] Finally, he replaced the noisy calling over of names at the end of each service with a silent and orderly retirement by the boys under his attentive eye.

His preaching, however, Sunday by Sunday was his most characteristic activity. Through it he gradually established his hold on the boys' loyalty and affection, and through the publication of selections of his sermons, which filled five volumes in his lifetime and were read by many, including Queen Victoria, his name and the school's have ever since been inseparably joined. Many, if not most, public-school headmasters and some boys still believe that the chapel lies at the heart of their school.

Not all, however, would agree with Arnold that chapel services should be compulsory. Compelling boys to attend for worship is thought by some to make a mockery of its essential nature and to be likely to be counter-productive in exciting their rebellious spirits. Yet a reasonable case, even in the post-Christian modern world, can be made out for compulsory chapel. There is much in the view of William Temple, former Headmaster of Repton and Archbishop of Canterbury, that boys have 'a strongly mystical tendency' which 'should be appealed to and developed'.[24] The most obvious place for this development is the school chapel. Why, moreover, should a school allow one particular activity which it regards as most important for its pupils' long-term future to be voluntary when with most other activities regarded as important it has no scruples about requiring attendance?

Whether chapel attendance is compulsory or voluntary (and in many public schools today it is voluntary or at least optional), most modern headmasters of these schools still regard preaching to their boys at least once a term, usually at a compulsory service, as an essential and important duty. That this should be so and that public schools still take a lively interest in religious worship must, in large measure, be credited to Arnold, who showed how valuable such preaching and services can be.

5

TEACHING

Arnold's work as headmaster and his work as teacher of the Sixth Form were so closely blended that it is difficult to speak of them apart.[1] Arnold indeed believed most strongly that moral and spiritual influences should be brought to bear on the training of the intellect and should control it. 'There are two parts of our nature, which are in a manner the very seeds of eternal life:—our feelings of humility and love. What will become of us if the strong and intense pursuit after intellectual excellence smothers these?'[2] He regarded school work as primarily educative rather than, as his predecessors, largely instructive. It prepared pupils for citizenship, encouraging them to promote the well-being of society.

It was this belief that made him spend so much time on personally teaching the Sixth Form: it was this that inspired his best pupils. Although he used the classical authors, particularly the historians and philosophers, as the main medium of his instruction, he was not himself an exact linguistic scholar of the first rank, inferior to Dr Butler of Shrewsbury in this respect and, in the view of his pupil W. C. Lake, to his immediate predecessor Dr Wooll. At Oxford he had won the Chancellor's prize for Latin and English essays, but failed to win a University prize for Latin Verse. As Mr Justice Coleridge, his Corpus contemporary and close friend, wrote later, 'he did not leave the College with scholarship proportioned to his great abilities and opportunities', and he undervalued 'those niceties of language, the intimate acquaintance with which he did not then perceive to be absolutely necessary to a precise knowledge of the meaning of the author'.[3] He understood the general structure of sentences and general principles of language, but in composing Latin and Greek saw little merit in the cultivation of style for its own sake. Yet he thought prose composition had some value, not only as the best way to gain knowledge of the classical writers but also as a means of improving accuracy in the use of English.[4]

He was indeed much better equipped to teach history than the classical languages. From his earliest years he had been fascinated by the subject and had had his historical imagination stirred by his observation, from his home in the Isle of Wight, of British ships sailing to do battle in the Napoleonic War. At the age of 3 he was reading Smollett's *History of England*, at 8 Dr Priestley's *Lectures on History*, at Winchester, as we have seen, he read through Gibbon twice, at Oxford Herodotus and Thucydides were among his favourite authors, and at Laleham he had come under the German historian Niebuhr's spell.

So unlike most teachers of the classics of his day, Arnold enjoyed using the ancient texts both to understand the past *and* to draw lessons for the present. 'The knowledge of the past', he wrote, 'is valuable because without it our knowledge of the present and of the future must be scanty: but if the knowledge of the past be confined wholly to itself, if instead of being made to bear upon things around us, it be totally isolated from them, and so disguised by vagueness and misapprehension as to appear incapable of illustrating them, then indeed it becomes little better than laborious trifling and they who declaim against it may be fully forgiven.'[5] Greek and Roman history, he wrote, are 'a living picture of things present, fitted not so much for the curiosity of the scholar as for the instruction of the statesman and the citizen'.[6] Yet he was well aware of the dangers involved in drawing lessons from the past.[7]

Though he may well be criticized for having, in G. M. Young's words, 'led us back with firm hand to the unchangeable routine of the Renaissance', for not breaking away from the traditional classical curriculum, he had one effective defence, namely that, while there were many who could teach it, 'there was hardly anyone who could teach anything else'.[8] That he would have liked to introduce more modern authors such as Dante and Goethe is clear from a letter of September 1836 to Mr Justice Coleridge.[9]

Even if he had no specially new methods or techniques in the teaching of classics, no fundamentally new curriculum, at least he had a new and much broader approach. His obvious delight in teaching, the enthusiasm and freshness with which he drew analogies between ancient and modern times, his understanding of his pupils' intellectual and moral concerns, excited their love of learning and stimulated them to think for themselves.[10] His religious approach to all study and his fertile historical imagination brought their history lessons to life and made them appear relevant to the present. 'No direct instruction', wrote Stanley,

could leave on their minds a livelier image of his disgust at moral evil than the black cloud of indignation which passed over his face when speaking of the crimes of Napoleon, or of Caesar, and the dead pause which followed, as if the acts had just been committed in his very presence. No expression of his reverence for a high standard of Christian excellence could have been more striking than the almost involuntary expressions of admiration which broke from him whenever mention was made of St Louis of France. . . . No more forcible contrast could have been drawn between the value of Christianity and of heathenism, than the manner with which, for example, after reading in the earlier part of the lesson one of the Scripture descriptions of the Gentile world, 'Now', he said, as he opened the *Satires* of Horace, 'we shall see what it was.'[11]

He was adept at finding connections between one period and another and drawing appropriate lessons from them. These would be either superficial similarities described for the sake of entertainment or genuine historical analogies between similar developments at the same stage in the history of two countries. He would ask, for instance, 'for the chief events which occurred . . . in the year 15 of two or three successive centuries, and, by making the boys contrast or compare them together bring before their minds the differences and resemblances in the state of Europe in each of the periods in question'.[12] 'Can you get for me', he wrote on another occasion to his friend the Archbishop of Dublin on 25 November 1836, 'and send me a good Erse grammar; and that book that you were mentioning, about the Welsh being Picts, and not the Aborigines of Wales? I shall want all this for the Gallic invasion of Rome; so beautifully does History branch out into all varieties of questions, and continually lead one into fresh fields of knowledge.'[13]

Military history and topography were special interests of his with which he enlivened his teaching. His interest in warfare deepened through his life. He was always eager to visit battlefields and discuss tactics: on a tour of Italy he first went to survey the country round Lake Trasimene and Cannae; late in life he walked over the ground at Naseby with Carlyle, and studied Wellington's campaign against Soult in the Pyrenees. He constantly urged his pupils to keep a map beside them when reading history and was always quick to use diagrams and pictures to illustrate his lessons.[14]

Stanley enjoyed his teaching of history most,[15] but even with the more literary aspects of the classics, such as the translation into and out of Latin and Greek, Arnold managed to convey more than the mere mechanics of the languages. In the *Quarterly Journal of Education* for 1834 he set out his approach:

There are exercises in Composition in Greek and Latin prose, Greek and Latin Verse, and English prose as in other large classical schools. In the subjects given for original composition in the higher forms there is considerable variety,—historical descriptions of any remarkable events, geographical descriptions of countries, imaginary speeches and letters supposed to be spoken or written on some great question, or under some memorable circumstances; etymological accounts of words in different languages, and criticisms on different books are found to offer an advantageous variety to the essays on moral subjects, to which the boys' prose composition has sometimes been confined.[16]

He refused to set such traditional themes as 'Virtus est bona res'; any moral topics he set in a new form, not 'carpe diem' but 'carpere diem, jubent Epicurei, jubet hoc idem Christus'.[17]

An appendix in Stanley's *Life* lists some of the subjects that Arnold set his pupils for composition in Greek or Latin: conversation between Thomas Aquinas, James Watt, and Sir Walter Scott; the principal events and men of England, France, Germany, and Holland, AD 1600; a description of Oxford through the eyes of a resurrected Herodotus (in Greek); the ideal is superior to the real; the history of the province of Africa from the Roman conquest till modern times.[18]

From these topics and many others his teaching can be seen to have been imaginative and testing. He was a humanist in wishing to study the ancient civilizations through their languages rather than the languages for their own sake.[19] Boys in class were made to translate fluently into idiomatic English. Literal word-for-word construe was frowned on. Every lesson in Greek or Latin was also a lesson in English. 'The translation of every sentence in Demosthenes or Tacitus is properly an exercise in extemporaneous English composition; a problem how to express with equal brevity, clearness and force, in our own language, the thought which the original author has so admirably expressed in his.'[20] The best pupils were encouraged to reproduce the effect of the original in English, for example by translating Thucydides in the style of Bacon. As for versification he started by despising it as artificial, calling it a 'contemptible prettiness of the understanding', but by

October 1833 he was writing to Coleridge that he had begun to see its value. It was a counter to 'the mere fact system that would cram a boy with knowledge of particular things and call it information'. 'My own lessons with the Sixth Form are directed now . . . to the furnishing rules or formulae for them to work with . . . principles of taste as to the choice of English words, as to the keeping or varying idioms and metaphors.'[21]

His method of instruction was Socratic: he taught by questioning, eliciting rather than giving information. He did not aim to teach the boys knowledge but how to gain it. Stanley describes the process:

> As a general rule, he never gave information, except as a kind of reward for an answer, and often withheld it altogether, or checked himself in the very act of uttering it, from a sense that those whom he was addressing had not sufficient interest or sympathy to entitle them to receive it. His explanations were as short as possible—enough to dispose of the difficulty and no more; and his questions were of a kind to call the attention of the boys to the real point of every question and to disclose to them the exact boundaries of what they knew or did not know. With regard to younger boys, he said 'It is a great mistake to think that they should *understand* all they learn; for God has ordered that in youth the memory should act vigorously, independent of the understanding, whereas a man cannot recollect a thing unless he understands it.' But in proportion to their advance in the school he tried to motivate in them a habit not only of collecting facts, but of expressing themselves with facility, and of understanding the principles on which their facts rested. 'You come here', he said, 'not to read, but to learn how to read.'[22]

There were no histrionics in his teaching. Sitting in the Upper Bench room, with its gallery and book-lined walls, in an 'undignified kitchen chair', he was modest enough to admit mistakes or confess ignorance, to ask the boys for help or information.[23] The good teacher, he believed, must always be learning, 'for it is ill drinking out of a pond whose stock of water is merely the remains of the long-past rains of the winter and spring'.[24] Although he accepted his pupils' correction or assistance, he was nevertheless a strict disciplinarian; he could not tolerate idleness or inattention. 'The pleased look and the cheerful "Thank you" which followed upon a successful answer or translation were just as surely replaced by the severe look and sudden "sit down" which followed upon the reverse.'[25] He treated the Sixth Form as equals as long as all went well. He would join in their laughter where there was good cause, but he would at once check the slightest sign of levity or impertinence. Aware of his irascibility he used to dismiss boys from the room—a most undesirable pedagogic practice—if they misbehaved at all, for he did not trust himself in such circumstances to act with restraint. This was indeed a weakness, but at least he recognized it and took precautions against succumbing to it. The lesson over and apology made, Arnold readily forgave.

To the boy Stanley writing home in 1831, when he had just joined the Sixth Form, Rugby without Arnold would have been a 'world without a sun', but by no means all boys were so magnetized.[26] One correspondent, who described Arnold's teaching at some length to the adult Stanley when the latter was writing his biography, criticized his temper, his overbearing views that had sometimes to be altered, his tendency to treat all pupils in the same way when variety of approach would on occasions have achieved better results (severity making some boys work hard but discouraging others from exertion), and at times an over-severe judgement of individual boys. Most of those in the Sixth Form, however, eulogized him.

Lower down the school he was regarded with extreme fear. Each week he took two lessons in forms below the Sixth, a practice initiated by Dr James but not carried out so methodically; these visits, too short to establish a worthwhile relationship, were awaited with keen interest but also dread, as Thomas Hughes's famous account of the *triste lupus* episode conveys:

Prayers and calling-over seemed twice as short as usual, and before they could get construes of a tithe of the hard passages marked in the margin of their books, they were all seated round, and the Doctor was standing in the middle, talking in whispers to the master. Tom couldn't hear a word which passed, and never lifted his eyes from his book; but he knew by a sort of magnetic instinct that the Doctor's under lip was coming out, and his eye beginning to burn, and his gown getting gathered up more and more tightly in his left hand. The suspense was agonizing, and Tom knew that he was sure on such occasions to make an example of the School-house boys. 'If he would only begin,' thought Tom, 'I shouldn't mind.'

At last the whispering ceased, and the name which was called out was not Brown. He looked up for a moment, but the Doctor's face was too awful; Tom wouldn't have met his eye for all he was worth, and buried himself in his book again.

The boy who was called up first was a clever merry School-house boy, one of their set: he was some connection of the Doctor's, and a great favourite, and ran in and out of his house as he liked, and so was selected for the first victim.

'Triste lupus stabulis,' began the luckless youngster, and stammered through some eight or ten lines.

'There, that will do,' said the Doctor; 'now construe.'

On common occasions the boy could have construed the passage well enough probably, but now his head was gone.

'Triste lupus, the sorrowful wolf,' he began.

A shudder ran through the whole form, and the Doctor's wrath fairly boiled over; he made three steps up to the construer, and gave him a good box on the ear. The blow was not a hard one, but the boy was so taken by surprise that he started back; the form caught the back of his knees, and over he went on to the floor behind. There was a dead silence over the whole school; never before and never again while Tom was at school did the Doctor strike a boy in lesson. The provocation must have been great. However, the victim had saved his form for that occasion, for the Doctor turned to the top bench, and put on the best boys for the rest of the hour; and though at the end of the lesson he gave them all such a rating as they did not forget, this terrible field-day passed over without any severe visitations in the shape of punishments or floggings. Forty young scapegraces expressed their thanks to the 'sorrowful wolf' in their different ways before second lesson.[27]

By these regular forays into the lower forms, though normally without such indefensible physical violence, Arnold saw every member of the school at work at least once each term, always in the company of their form master, who was thus put on his mettle too.

Two other developments of his predecessors' practices were his reintroduction of the Eton tutorial system in February 1840 and his institution of termly examinations of the whole school.[28] As in Dr James's time, the tutorial system required each boy to have private lessons with a tutor, preparing Latin or Greek construe, or showing him his compositions, before going into class.[29] Since less time was then needed for working out an accurate translation, more could be spent by the form master in discussing the passage's significance. So in theory classroom work became more interesting. The drawback was the duplication of labour, for which the main compensation was the personal relationship between master and boy which developed and continued throughout his school days. The most valuable aspect of the Eton system, private business, informal tutorial teaching in small groups, used by tutors to educate their charges generally, never took root at Rugby.

Under Dr Wooll the Sixth had sat an examination at the end of the school year, but this was now extended to the whole school. During the last three weeks of term every form was questioned in the school library by Arnold assisted by two masters. As further incentive to study he established, at his own expense, new form prizes, which were not restricted to the intelligent and successful. Plodders he was always anxious to encourage, and for these there were prizes for effort. In other ways also, perhaps by the gift of a book, he encouraged deserving individuals. The school as a whole he rewarded rather differently. From time to time, when he was pleased with the overall standard of work or when an Oxford or Cambridge scholarship was won, he gave the boys an extra half-holiday—an even more popular innovation.[30]

By these methods Arnold restored to Rugby the intellectual impetus that had been there in Dr James's day.[31] In answer to the charge that this was to the detriment of some boys who suffered from excessive premature exertion it may be said that, if he found a boy reading too much or overtired, he relaxed his demands or, if he were a Sixth-Former, invited him to Fox How. By 1838 the school's reputation for scholarship had been more than fully recovered, and the happy coincidence of this academic success with the opening of the railway on 17 September soon led to the great increase in numbers of his last three years.

By these methods also he got to know his boys, and soon after his appointment, in 1829, he evidently thought that he knew enough about each to start the practice of writing a half-yearly report to his parents.[32] Within a year the form masters' comments were also added. Later still, towards the end of his time, so concerned was he to keep parents in touch with their sons' development that he sent reports home as often as every month, for unlike today parents never or very rarely saw their children during term. All these useful practices have long become normal in public schools, and only in the largest of these, such as Eton and Marlborough, does the headmaster no longer write reports on all the boys himself. There the housemaster fulfils that role.

Arnold's approach to the teaching of classics has been described, and it was on classics in a broad sense that most time in school was spent. Sixteen of the twenty lessons each week, which varied in length from one to one-and-three-quarter hours, were devoted to them, though these included scripture, geography, and history, ancient and modern. So the curriculum was not as narrow as it might at first glance appear and as it has sometimes been considered. Indeed the Rugby curriculum which Arnold set out in full in the article in the *Quarterly Journal of Education*[33] already referred to has been called by another headmaster of today a masterpiece. It was certainly well planned and received favourable comment from the Clarendon Commissioners of 1864. It showed no major innovations, but provided a more liberal education than Rubgy's main rivals.[34] For, apart from the untraditional way in which Arnold taught the classics, the only new features were the greater amount of modern history, taught from up-to-date books, and the recognition of mathematics and modern languages as regular subjects. Arnold was not, however, original in introducing these developments. The commercial schools, which educated most of the middle classes, had already admitted into their curriculum mathematics, modern history, and geography, and Samuel Butler at Shrewsbury had likewise forestalled Arnold in teaching algebra and geometry, and some modern history.[35]

Arnold's personal album, kept during part of his headmastership, records against 6 July 1830 the note, in his own hand: 'By an order of the same date the appointment of a Mathematical Master and a Master of Modern languages was confirmed: these two Masters to rank in all respects on an equality with the Classical Assistant Masters, and the study of Mathematics, and that of Modern languages, being made a regular Part of the Business of the School.'[36]

Mathematics had been taught in Dr James's day by the headmaster himself since it was his hobby, but he found teaching it, for an hour a week after formal business on Saturday mornings, a great strain, at times even painful. Gradually it came to be taught on the side by part-time assistants, so that its full-scale recognition as a proper school subject by Arnold was a significant, if limited, step. Unable to teach beyond the first six books of Euclid, he nevertheless had a strong sense of its importance and beauty.[37] Even so, the Sixth Form went no further than trigonometry, and did not attempt calculus.

French had of course also been taught long before Arnold, at least as early as 1779, but its teaching had been in the hands of part-time specialists and paid for by parents as an extra. Now one of the permanent staff was made responsible, and two hours each week were allocated to the subject. German, not hitherto taught in schools at all, was introduced after 1835, not so much to enable boys to speak the language as to understand the many works of classical scholarship written by Germans which they would need to read at university. Arnold himself regretted that he had not learnt German at school. A letter to Hawtrey in October 1834 congratulating him on his appointment as Head Master of Eton and one in 1840 to the Earl of Denbigh, the Chairman of the Trustees, make his policy on modern languages abundantly clear. It is an attitude that has bedevilled the public-school attitude to language teaching for far too long. 'We can teach French and German as we do Latin and Greek, and that I think is the great object as a matter of liberal education. Fluency in speaking is undoubtedly a great matter of convenience when a man goes abroad, but I do not think it should be our object here, even if it were not, as it clearly is, unattainable at a public school under any system.'

I assume it certainly as the foundation of all my view of the case, that boys at a public school will never learn to speak or pronounce French well under any circumstances. But to most of our boys, to read it will be of far more use than to speak it; and if they learn it grammatically as a dead language, I am sure that whenever they may have any occasion to speak it, as in going abroad, for instance, they will be able to do it very rapidly. I think that if we can enable the boys to read French with facility, and to know the grammar well, we shall do as much as can be done at a public school, and should teach the boys something valuable. And, in point of fact, I have heard men, who have left Rugby, speak with gratitude of what they learnt with us in French and German.

It is very true that our general practice here, as in other matters, does not come up to our theory; and I know too well that most of the boys would pass a very poor examination even in French grammer. But so it is with their mathematics; and so it will be with any branch of knowledge that is taught but seldom, and is felt to be quite subordinate to the boy's main study. Only I am quite sure that if the boy's regular masters fail in this, a foreigner, be he who he may, would fail much more.

I do not therefore see any way out of the difficulties of the question, and I believe sincerely that our present plan is the *least bad*, I will not say *the best*, that can be adopted; discipline is not injured as it is with foreign masters, and I think that something is taught, though but little. With regard to German, I can speak more confidently; and I am sure that there we do facilitate a boy's after-study of the language considerably, and enable him, with much less trouble, to read those many German books, which are so essential to his classical studies at the university.[38]

The Clarendon Commissioners judged Arnold's plan for modern language teaching a failure. However, still more glaring deficiencies of the Arnold curriculum are the absence of English and of the natural sciences. But Arnold was at pains to teach his pupils through the languages of Greek and Latin how to use their own. In his *Quarterly Journal* article he 'argued that the study of Greek and Latin considered as mere languages is of importance mainly as it enables us to understand and employ well that language in which we commonly think, and speak, and write'.[39] It may be said in his defence that English literature was not then studied in class in any public school, and that this continued to be so until well on into this century.

His omission of the natural sciences was equally deliberate, for he had inherited from his predecessors a sixty-year-old scheme of triennial science lectures, with special emphasis on physics, given by the Walker family, father and son.[40] Adam, the father, had initiated these as far back as the mid-1770s, but though they were so well established and could scarcely in the time allowed them have distracted the boys from their main subjects, Arnold insisted that those who wanted to attend them should have their parents' written permission or themselves pay the guinea fee, and firmly discouraged Adam's son from continuing them, perhaps because he was showing signs of being past his prime. His last, abortive, visit took place in 1837.[41]

Arnold was not in fact against the subject, only concerned that it should not compete with those he thought more important. He thought it 'only fit for earning a livelihood, of no educationai significance as a preparative for power'. 'Physical Science', he told the Mechanics' Institute at Rugby in 1838, 'alone can never make a man educated; even the formal sciences, invaluable as they are with respect to the discipline of the reasoning powers, cannot instruct the judgment; it is only moral and religious knowledge which can accomplish this.'[42] While he shrank personally from the study of natural history as 'one of such painful mystery that I dare not approach it',[43] he was fascinated by geology and twice attended geological discussions at British Association meetings in Birmingham. Moreover, as two letters to former pupils show, he wished that there was time for teaching the physical sciences. He wrote to an old pupil, Dr Greenhill, on 9 May 1836:

If one might wish for impossibilities, I might then wish that my children might be well versed in physical science, but in due subordination to the fulness and freshness of their knowledge on moral subjects. This, however, I believe cannot be; and physical science, if studied at all, seems too great to be studied εν παρέργῳ: wherefore, rather than have it the principal thing in my son's mind, I would gladly have him think that the sun went round the earth, and that the stars were so many spangles set in the bright blue firmament. Surely the one thing needful for a Christian and an Englishman to study is Christian and moral and political philosophy, and then we should see our way a little more clearly without falling into Judaism or Toryism or Jacobinism or any other *ism* whatever.[44]

Yet a letter written towards the end of his life (to the Revd Herbert Hill, 8 May, 1840) suggests that he had revised his views:

. . . I do really think that with boys and young men it is not right to leave them in ignorance of the beginnings of physical science. It is so hard to begin anything in after life and so comparatively easy to continue what has been begun, that I think we are bound to break ground, as it were, into several of the mines of knowledge with our pupils, that the first difficulties may be overcome by them while there is yet a power from without to aid their own faltering resolution, and that so they may be enabled, if they will, to go on with the study thereafter.[45]

Arnold's own Wykehamist and Oxford education prevented his having any vision of science as a major area of knowledge, of which all boys should have some understanding. In his view, a liberal education was not to be gained through the accumulation of facts about the natural world, however interesting in themselves. The education given by science was essentially vocational. Boys might be encouraged to engage in such enquiries during their leisure hours, but could not expect to gain from them the intellectual exercise, excitement, and benefit or the moral and political insights that they would from the classics and religion properly taught. In Arnold's lifetime such a neglect of the natural sciences was common among the public and endowed schools. Today the pendulum has swung so far the other way that some may consider his assessment of priorities to be less misguided than Strachey and other critics have thought.

If, however, it is true that, as Correlli Barnett has argued, Arnold was 'more responsible than any other single person for the nature of late Victorian élite education',[46] he can with some justice be blamed for the baneful effect that his advocacy of a liberal education had on England's attitude to industry and technical subjects. His view was that vocational training did not cultivate the mind and inspire the moral sense. Only 'useless' subjects like the classics and divinity could do that. But in his defence it must be said that Arnold was by no means alone in his outlook: Cardinal Newman expressed influentially, and even more strongly, similar thoughts in *The Idea of a University*, and headmasters before Arnold like Samuel Butler at Shrewsbury (1798–1836) and Dr Vicesimus Knox at Tonbridge (1778–1812), to instance only two, had also based the education of their schools on the classics. That was the unexceptionable norm, until at least the 1830s, and Arnold was not an original enough thinker on education to break away from it. In fact the strength of his convictions was such that he did more than most nineteenth-century headmasters to reinforce an attitude towards education that, though in many respects valuable, was finally too narrow and limiting.[47]

6

DISCIPLINE

Arnold was a good but not a great teacher. Even his most devoted admirer Stanley conceded that. Asked by Dr Percival, a later Head Master of Rugby, how much he had learnt in the Sixth Form under Arnold, Stanley held up a small notebook which he had in his hand and said that it could contain the lot.[1] W. C. Lake, another admirer, considered his headmaster's teaching earnest and honest but not profound, his mind vigorous and clear rather than subtle or comprehensive.[2] Arnold made his name not by teaching but by what he made of Rugby as a community. His single-minded determination to make it a Christian school, his efforts to improve its moral tone, inspired his public attitudes and decisions. Rebuking the boys on one occasion he said: 'Is this a Christian school? I cannot remain here if all is to be carried on by constraint and force; if I am to be here as a gaoler, I will resign my office at once.' At another time, when he had stirred up a spirit of rebellion by expelling several boys at once, he told the assembled school, 'It is *not* necessary that this should be a school of three hundred, or one hundred, or fifty boys; but it *is* necessary that it should be a school of Christian gentlemen.'[3]

He saw himself as constantly at war with the devil, checking the vices of individual boys and, more particularly, trying to create an atmosphere in which evil was abhorred by the school as a whole.[4] Although he doubted the value of boarding and hesitated whether to send his own sons away to Winchester, he nevertheless believed that membership of a *great* school could be a fine preparation for life.[5] One of his Founder's Day sermons (Vol. III, XVI) gives this philosophy forceful expression:

It seems to me that there is, or ought to be, something very ennobling in being connected with any establishment at once ancient and magnificent, where all about us and all the associations belonging to the objects around us should be great, splendid, and elevating. What an individual ought to derive, and often does derive, from the feeling that he is born of an old and illustrious race, from being familiar from his childhood with the walls and with the trees that speak of the past no less than of the present, and make both full of images of greatness, this in an inferior degree belongs to every member of an ancient and celebrated place of education. In this respect every one has a responsibility imposed upon him, which I wish that we more considered. We know how school traditions are handed down from one school generation to another, and what is it, if in all these there shall be nothing great, nothing distinguished, nothing but a record, to say the best of it, of mere boyish amusements, when it is not a record of boyish follies? Every generation in which a low and foolish spirit prevails does its best to pollute the local influences of the place, to deprive the thought of belonging to it of anything that may enkindle and ennoble the minds of those who come after it. And if these foolish or tame associations continue, they make the evil worse; persons who appreciate highly the elevating influence of a great and ancient foundation will no longer send their sons to a place which has forfeited one of its most valuable powers, whose antiquity has nothing of the dignity, nothing of the romance, of antiquity, but is either blank or worse than a blank. So the spirit gets lower and lower, and instead of finding a help and an encouragement in the association of its place of education, the ingenuous mind feels them all no more than a weight upon its efforts; they only tend to thwart it and keep it down. This is the tendency not only of a vicious tone, but even of a foolish and childish one, of a tone that tolerates ignorance and an indifference about all save the amusements of the day. On the other hand, whatever is done here well and honourably, outlives its own generation. . . . The size, the scale, the wealth, of a great institution like this ensures its permanency, so far as anything on earth is permanent. The good and the evil, the nobleness or the vileness, which may exist on this ground now, will live and breathe here in the days of our children; they will form the atmosphere in which they will live hereafter, either wholesome and invigorating, or numbing and deadly.

The creation of such a community depended on the relationship of the highest form to the rest of the boys.[6] By the highest form he meant the thirty boys who composed the Sixth Form, those who, having risen

to the highest form in the school . . . will probably be at once the oldest, and the strongest, and the cleverest; and . . . if the school be well ordered, the most respectable in application and general character . . . their business is to keep order among the boys; to put a stop to improprieties of conduct, especially to prevent . . . oppression and ill-usage of the weaker boys by the stronger. . . . For all these purposes a general authority over the rest of the school is given them. . . . This governing part of the school, thus invested with great responsibility, treated by the masters with great confidence and consideration, and being constantly in direct communication with the head master and receiving their instruction almost exclusively from him, learn to feel a corresponding self-respect in the best sense of the term; they look upon themselves as answerable for the character of the school and by the natural effect of their position acquire a manliness of mind and habits of conduct infinitely superior, generally speaking, to those of young men of the same age who have not enjoyed the same advantages.[7]

He saw the Sixth as intermediaries between the masters and the mass of the boys who would 'transmit, through their example and influence, right principles of conduct instead of those extremely low ones which are natural to a society of boys left wholly to form their own standard of right and wrong';[8] '. . . my great desire is to teach my boys to govern themselves—a much better thing than to govern them well myself. Only in their case "*propter defectum aetatis*" . . . they never can be quite able to govern themselves, and will need some of my government.'[9]

It is for his reliance on these boys to create such respect for moral and intellectual excellence and to control the day-to-day discipline, for his development of what has become known as the prefect system, that he is best known. How far was this an original innovation? What were its essential characteristics? How successful was it?

There was nothing new in giving older boys responsibility. Praepostors, monitors, prefects, call them what you will, older boys helping the headmaster, with some authority and powers of punishment, are to be found in schools long before the nineteenth century.[10] In Winchester's fourteenth-century Statutes there is mention of older boys superintending the younger, and by the seventeenth there were prefects there with specific duties. Eton had eighteen praepostors in the sixteenth century, Westminster had them in the seventeenth century, and Dr James, on moving from Eton to Rugby in 1778, had introduced praepostors on Etonian lines, giving the Sixth Form boys an authority that was mainly formal. Under Dr Wooll this authority, greatly increased, had become a real influence for good. At Shrewsbury Dr Butler earlier than Arnold also developed the monitorial system by making more use of his praepostors than had been customary. They had a 'quasi-independent part in the government of the School and the maintenance of good conduct'.[11] Arnold himself attributed to his own headmaster, Goddard (Winchester, 1796–1809), his system of government by senior boys.

What was new was the extent to which he used his prefects, his Sixth Form, to transmit his influence throughout the school, the depth of his trust in them. They were to be much more than an 'efficient engine of discipline', though they were that too.[12] He expected them to keep order, check bullying, punish boys found drinking spirits, visiting pubs, or smoking, and he fully supported against strong criticism from parents and newspapers their right to cane boys below the Fifth Form. Miscreants could, however, appeal against an individual praepostor either to the Sixth Form as a whole or to the headmaster.[13]

But their responsibilities went far wider than the routine administration of discipline. They were to help him to create a Christian society; they were fellow-workers with him, concerning themselves with religious and moral principles first, and with boys' behaviour only secondarily. That this exalted concept of their role was accepted by many members of his Sixth Form is clear from the memoirs of men such as A. H. Clough ('I verily believe that my whole being is soaked through with watching and hoping and striving to do the school good'),[14] C. J. Vaughan, and W. C. Lake, and the biography of Dean Stanley. A twentieth-century Head Master of Eton is attributed with the cynical remark, 'If you trust boys, they will let you down. If you don't trust them, they will do you down.' That the boys' response to Arnold's trust was not always wholeheartedly complete is suggested by his remark in one of his farewell talks to leavers: 'When I have confidence in the Sixth, there is no post in England which I would exchange for this; but if they do not support me, I must go.'[15]

That his development of the prefect system is rightly regarded as one of his particular achievements is perhaps best shown by its imitations at other schools in the second half of the nineteenth century by those who had served on his staff at Rugby or been his pupils. A prime example is Marlborough under George Cotton, the 'young master' in *Tom Brown's Schooldays*, who was a member of the Rugby staff from 1837 to 1852. Founded in 1843, by 1851 the school was out of control. Cotton was appointed to restore order, and at once introduced a prefect system. His talk to the school when this innovation was opposed made his attitude clear:

The Council informed me on my appointment that the school was in a bad state of discipline, and they hoped that I would allow no boy to go out except in pairs under a master. I told them I could not accept office on such terms, that the school I hoped to govern was a public school, not a private one, and I would try to govern it by means of prefects. The school knows now how matters stand. They must either submit to the prefects or be reduced to the level of a private school and have their freedom ignominiously curtailed. The prefects are and shall be, as long as I am Head, the governors of the school. As soon as I see that this is impracticable, I shall resign.[16]

Rossall (1844), Wellington (1859), Haileybury (1862), and Clifton (1862) show similarly striking Arnoldian influence. Chapter 9 will show why this was so.

Though Arnold's prefect system was not self-government, it undoubtedly gave the senior boys an exaggerated sense of their own importance, and this premature responsibility tended to make at least some of them prigs.[17] Sir Francis Doyle put this criticism well: Arnold forgot that it was 'God Almighty's intention that there should exist . . . between childhood and manhood the natural production known as a boy.'[18] Arnold might well have replied by saying that if senior boys are not persuaded to help in the government of a school, the burden of government falls fully on the headmaster himself, and his staff.

With hindsight, too, it is easy today to be critical of Arnold for allowing his Sixth Form to enforce discipline by the use of corporal punishment. A form of punishment which is now widely recognized as open to abuse, even by adults, should not have been entrusted to adolescents. But at the time its use was so widespread in schools that modern inhibitions about it would have seemed unreasonable. He could not have foreseen that senior boys would continue for more than a hundred years after his death to have this power of beating younger boys or the unfortunate effect that it sometimes had, particularly on the older boys who administered this form of punishment. He had no reason to know that this power was abused in his time, as George Melly, who joined Rugby as a pupil in 1840, described in his memoirs ('I was flogged twice a week regularly by the monitor'), or that it would continue to be abused from time to time thereafter.

In other ways also the prefect system that was adopted by schools elsewhere lost its particular Arnoldian character. Prefects retained their authority and powers but the emphasis moved steadily to using these simply for purposes of discipline rather than to create a Christian community.

Nor should Arnold be criticized for aiming to turn out leaders in the world at large. Not only is he on record as being opposed to the recruitment to Rugby of the sons of leading families, but there is also no suggestion in Stanley's biography, or in the views of Arnold's friends and pupils there quoted, that he prepared his boys for such leadership. Most of them looked to Church, School, or University for their life's work rather than to high positions in politics, government, or society.

Fagging, Arnold thought, was as essential as prefects to the good government of a large boarding-school, as he made clear in his discussion of it in 1835:

> By 'the power of fagging' I understand a power given by the supreme authorities of a school to the boys of the highest class or classes in it, to be exercised by them over the lower boys for the sake of securing the advantages of regular government amongst the boys themselves, and avoiding the evils of anarchy,—in other words, of the lawless tyranny of physical strength . . . an institution . . . often abused and requires to be carefully watched, but . . . indispensable to a multitude of boys living together . . .[19]

He allowed only the thirty members of the Sixth Form, however, to have fags, and provided that they used their privilege moderately, he never intervened to excuse a fag some duty imposed by his seniors. As Tom Brown described them, these were usually not unpleasant or arduous: answering fag-calls in the evenings to fetch beer or bread and cheese for a praepostor, cleaning candlesticks, toasting cheese, bottling beer, carrying messages about the house; in the mornings after breakfast cleaning out his praepostor's study, and in return for this service having access to 'the great men's studies, and looking at their pictures, and peeping into their books'. Yet there was another side to this, mentioned by Thomas Hughes in a memoir of his brother George, where he wrote that small boys were often fagged for every moment of their play hours day after day.[20]

Arnold's restriction of the number of those entitled to fags was all part of his campaign against bullying, and though we know from Tom Brown's roasting by Flashman that bullying continued in Arnold's time, it was much reduced. 'The sharpest chastisement that Dr Arnold ever inflicted was for this offence.'[21]

The Sixth were enjoined to report unauthorized fagging immediately to Arnold, and a second offence of this sort by the same boy led to expulsion. So effective was this policy that within a year of his arrival an unathletic new boy of scholarly tastes, his later biographer Stanley, could write to his Carthusian brother, 'my first entrance into a public school was far more agreeable than yours. . . . There is very little fagging and no bullying except smoking thro' the study doors.'[22] (Boys blew smoke through the keyholes to try to force those inside to come out.) George Melly's memoirs, too, commended the practice of fagging, although he himself fagged for three and a half years and never rose high enough in the school to qualify for a fag himself.[23]

A proper, well-regulated system of fagging, Arnold argued, protected the weak from being bullied or put upon, enabled necessary services to be carried out for those most deserving, not simply the strongest, and gave junior boys quickness, helpfulness, punctuality, and powers of endurance, all valuable in later life. Though the system could be improved, he was set against its abolition.[24]

Perhaps as important to the creation of a healthy tone in the school as the relationship between senior and junior boys was Arnold's striking ability to communicate his thoughts and feelings to the school as a whole. In formal assemblies in 'the great school', when he would address them all on some matter of discipline, or week by week on Sundays in chapel, he conveyed his views with trenchant force.[25]

What he disliked most was the boys' moral insensitivity. He longed for them to abhor evil as he did, and the absence of such abhorrence he attributed to 'combination', deference to public opinion in the school, what today would be called peer-group loyalty.[26] A young boy's transition from a good home to school required great moral courage if he were not to debase the standards set by his family. Laziness and vice too readily and rapidly replaced innocence and decency. One of his sermons well expressed this deep anxiety of his:

> You see a number of boys who, while living at home, or by themselves, might get on very well, and think and act very rightly, yet, as soon as they mix with one another, and form one large body, the opinions and influence on that body shall be bad. Every boy brings some good with him, at least, from home, as well as some evil; and yet you see how very much more catching the evil is than the good.[27]

He saw this group spirit as undermining his authority and his efforts to develop close relations between the boys and himself.[28] The sight of a group of boys gathered round the School House fire made him think that he saw the devil in their midst. Two boys seen walking together, whom he had not so observed before, would make him suspicious. 'I never saw them together before,' he said to a new master. 'You should make an especial point of observing the company they keep:—nothing so tells the changes in a boy's character.'[29] (Many modern headmasters and housemasters would agree.) Indeed, although he did not see much of the boys in the lower part of the school, he claimed to know pretty well how they were developing, and though his character assessments were sometimes mistaken, most boys thought that he understood them well.[30] The Sixth Form of course saw most of him, and he made as many opportunities as he could, inside and outside the classroom, to get to know them individually. The Fifth Form, too, he made more responsible and respectable by reducing their number to about two dozen.

The sixty to seventy boys who boarded in School House he of course knew much better. There were so many more opportunities to get on terms with them; in particular, in preparing them for confirmation, or spending an hour or so in the evening on private conversation with individual boys. House Prayers each evening he attended also, unless prevented, having introduced soon after his arrival at Rugby the practice of reading from the Bible himself whenever he was present.[31] At the beginning and towards the end of his headmastership he gave a short address as well on these occasions.

In such positive ways did he communicate his values and beliefs to his pupils, but inevitably he had also to punish miscreants. Stanley assures us that in the upper part of the school he tried to keep punishment as such in the background and appealed to the boys' better nature. He would shame them by words, often reducing even the older ones to tears, rather than punish.[32] 'I believe', he wrote to the Revd F. C. Blackstone in September 1828,

> that boys may be governed a great deal by gentle methods and kindness . . . if you show that you are not afraid of them; I have seen great boys, six feet high, shed tears when I have sent for them up into my room and spoken to them quietly, in private, for not knowing their lesson, and I found that this treatment produced its effects afterwards, in making them do better. But,

of course, deeds must second words when needful, or words will soon be laughed at.[33]

Younger boys he flogged, for such offences as lying, drinking, habitual idleness. Though he claimed to be averse from inflicting corporal punishment and Stanley says that it was less often used than might have been expected, it is not easy to be sure where the truth lies. In support of Stanley's view is the description of his policy in a letter dated 5 April 1829 to the Revd C. T. Longley, to whom he wrote to congratulate on his appointment as Head Master of Harrow:

I have so far got rid of the birch that I only flogged seven boys last half year and the same number hitherto in this. I never did nor do I believe that it can be relinquished altogether—but I think it may well be reserved for offences either great in themselves or rendered great by frequent repetition: and then it should be administered in earnest.[34]

On the other hand, his letter to George Cornish (30 November 1827), written when he was a candidate for Rugby, might be taken as indicating a different attitude:

. . . with God's blessing I should like to try whether my notions of Christian education are really impracticable, whether our system of public schools has not in it some noble elements which . . . might produce fruit even to life eternal. When I think about it thus, I really long to take rod in hand.[35]

Were it not that the rod was a traditional emblem of discipline associated with headmasters, and his reference to it more than probably shorthand for taking up a headmastership, we might think his self-confessed aversion from corporal punishment a pretence. No one today contemplating candidature for a headmaster's post would express his ambition in Arnold's terms.

He was indeed severely criticized in the local press during his time not only for personal brutality but also for the brutality of physical punishment administered by his Sixth Form.[36] In a long article in the *Quarterly Journal of Education* he defended the practice of corporal punishment. He refused to accept that it was degrading to the recipient; on the contrary it was appropriate to the inferior condition of boyhood. That it should be regarded as degrading sprang from a false notion of personal independence which was neither reasonable nor Christian, but essentially barbarian. Too much emphasis on the dignity of the individual had led to evils in the past and was doing the same in the present. Only the appeal to fear will move children. It was sin, not its punishment, that degraded.[37]

The March flogging incident, however, must surely be thought degrading.[38] Yet disgraceful though it was, it is evidence not of sadism so much as grossly intemperate behaviour. Just before the school broke up for the Christmas holidays, on one of his periodical visits to examine the academic progress of the lower forms, Arnold asked a boy called March to translate a passage from Xenophon's *Anabasis*. March claimed that the form had not prepared the translation of the text as far as this. He continued to deny it even after Arnold had checked the note given him by Mr Bird, the master who normally took the class and who was also his housemaster. So Arnold sent James Prince Lee, the young master who was accompanying him, to ask Bird whether he had made some mistake. The reply came back that Bird's note was correct, the boy wrong. Arnold regarded lying with special loathing. Persistent lying such as March's was indefensible. Without further enquiry from the rest of the class, who were presumably so terrified by this time by the Doctor's mien and manner that they dared not speak out in March's support, he mercilessly gave the boy eighteen strokes in front of them all.

March, a 14-year-old who had suffered from a hernia since the age of 3, was so shaken by his treatment that for two days he kept to his boarding-house. Arnold, accusing him of malingering, gave him extra work to make up for what he had missed. To us it seems odd that the boy did not ask his housemaster to intercede with the headmaster.

Then the news broke that Bird had been mistaken, and that the boy was innocent. Arnold immediately made a full apology, to the boy personally, to the class, to the boy before the whole school, and on the insistence of the parents, who had removed their son, a further written apology.

During the school holidays the Press got hold of the story. The account in the *Northampton Herald* for Saturday, 19 January 1833 was remarkably accurate, and on Arnold's return from Lakeland for the new term he found himself under severe public attack. Under his predecessors, James, Ingles, even Wooll, who, as we saw earlier, was thought to have used the rod too much, the *Herald* claimed no boy had ever received more than twelve strokes, and that was for open rebellion. If lying earned eighteen strokes, what was done to boys who committed more serious offences? A letter sent to the Press by eight members of the Rugby staff supporting their headmaster, with the assertion that, if the boy had been guilty of the offence attributed to him, he would have deserved the punishment that he received, served only to heighten the dismay. The staff's approval of such brutality confirmed the public's fears.

It is hard for us looking back not to feel horror at such treatment of a young boy. The only possible defence of Arnold's incontinent fury on that occasion is to stress his almost pathological hatred of lying. Central to his attitude to boys was his policy of treating them in personal relationships as adult, of encouraging them to respect themselves by the respect that he himself showed them. Lying to masters or to himself, therefore, he regarded as a cardinal moral offence. He would never have seen the force of C. S. Lewis's remark that schoolboys tell lies because it is their only form of defence against their masters. In this he was unusual. Dr Keate, Head Master of Eton, much respected by the boys, 'never minded his boys telling him a lie'. On the contrary, according to Lord Blachford, he 'exacted it as a mark of proper respect. I remember [when] in some trumpery scrape . . . I told him the literal truth; upon which he at once inquired of me, with a great appearance of anger, whether I had been drinking.'[39] To Arnold, on the other hand, lying was a major betrayal of trust. He normally always accepted a boy's word without hesitation: 'If you say so, that is quite enough—of course I believe your word.' So much was this so that boys felt 'it was a shame to tell Arnold a lie—he always believes one'.[40] Such headmasterly naïvety, admirable as it is in one respect, would be hard to find today.

So it was that when he found a boy lying, especially if this was persistent, he punished the malefactor severely. Senior boys he expelled for it, junior boys he flogged. It must be doubted whether others received such excessive punishment as March, yet the fact that it was almost certainly an isolated incident is no excuse. Such loss of temper and undeserved punishment of such extreme severity cannot plausibly be defended.

By contrast, Arnold's treatment of Tom Brown, as described by Thomas Hughes, most if not all of whose episodes are founded on fact, showed some understanding of adolescence. Having flogged him more than once for boyish offences such as poaching, without much evidence that his punishment had been effective, Arnold, rather than expel Tom, arranged, as we saw earlier, that at the start of the new school year he should share a study with a new boy, homesick and sensitive, who, having no father, found support in Tom and brought out the latter's fundamental goodness of heart and sense of responsibility.

Arnold's use of the rod, however, was not untypical of his age, and was accepted as normal by his boys. Where his disciplinary policy differed most from current practice, and is open to criticism today, was his attitude to expulsion or, as he preferred to call it, removal. He drew a clear distinction between the two: expulsion he regarded as the severest of punishments for the worst behaviour and a lasting disgrace, to be inflicted publicly and with great solemnity; this he used rarely.[41] This was altogether different from removal, which was a central plank of his policy, as he makes clear in his letter to his friend Dr Hawkins (21 October 1827), who was encouraging him to apply for the Rugby headmastership.

> According to my notions of what large schools are, founded on all I know and all I have ever heard of them, expulsion should be practised much oftener than it is. Now, I know that trustees, in general, are averse to this plan, because it has a tendency to lessen the numbers of the school, and they regard quantity more than quality. In fact, my opinions on this point might, perhaps, generally be considered as disqualifying me for the situation of master of a great school; yet I could not consent to tolerate much that I know is tolerated generally, and therefore, I should not like to enter on an office which I could not discharge according to my own means of what is right. I do not believe myself, that my system would be, in fact, a cruel or a harsh one, and I believe that with much care on the part of the masters, it would be seldom necessary to proceed to the *ratio ultima*; only I would have it clearly understood, that I would most unscrupulously resort to it, at whatever inconvenience, where there was a perseverance in any habit inconsistent with a boy's duties.[42]

'Sending away boys is a necessary and regular part of a good system,' he wrote to an assistant master, 'not as a punishment to one, but as a protection to others. Undoubtedly it would be a better system if there was no evil; but evil being unavoidable we are not a gaol to keep it in, but a place of education where we must cast it out, to prevent its taint from spreading.'[43] 'Till a man learns that the first, second, and third duty of a schoolmaster is to get rid of unpromising subjects, a great public school', he said, 'will never be what it ought to be.'[44]

From the outset he carried his policy into practice. He dispatched some twelve boys from his own House who, angered by the reforms that he was introducing, had stayed up one night to have a midnight carouse with pipes, wine, and spirits to discuss their hardships. Just as one of them remarked 'I wish the old black —— was here', the Doctor walked in. They all left the following morning.[45] On another occasion he expelled three boys for theft and sent four or five more away for two years, since they were so young that they might safely be admitted again by and by. He was determined to root out the wickedness he saw around him and make the school a place of education for good. He firmly believed the schoolmasterly cliché that only the removal of the rotten apples prevents the remainder in the barrel being spoilt. Such removal could be temporary or permanent, and often seemed to boys and parents arbitrary. Boys were allowed to stay whom their peers thought worthy of expulsion; others were dispatched for comparatively venial offences. As the years passed, he tended more and more to leave the removal of boys, especially those whose academic progress was inadequate, until the end of the half-year, when their departure would hardly be noticed, and he took great care to secure their subsequent education. He would recommend a private tutor or himself offer free tuition in the holidays. Later he would write to the head of an Oxford college commending his former pupil. Stanley gives several examples of such testimonials.[46]

That his policy was effective is clear from the steady increase in the school's numbers in his last years. Though some parents, especially those whose sons were removed, criticized his practice, most showed their support for it by sending their sons to him. The school they considered to be in a healthy condition.

Headmasters today are less ready to expel or remove, for several reasons: boarding-schools are not so disorderly or potentially rebellious; a much friendlier and more responsible atmosphere prevails; boys are treated much more as individuals needing to be understood; advances in the knowledge of child psychology have led to a more informed understanding of adolescent behaviour. Stealing, for instance, a common phenomenon in a boarding-house, often enough a cry for help or a sign of a loveless home, though clearly calling for a stern response, would nowadays not normally be punished by expulsion. The example of Thring, Headmaster of Uppingham in the second half of the nineteenth century, rather than that of Arnold is more often followed. Thring believed that a school should aim to educate *all* its pupils, drawing out in each boy his particular talent.

But some headmasters of the second half of the twentieth century are sometimes too soft-hearted. They would do better to adopt a more severe Arnoldian line and remove a boy who was a centre of disaffection or trouble. For there is much truth in the apple-barrel cliché. One bad apple soon blights the rest. The taint of rottenness in a boys' boarding community can still spread surprisingly fast and wreak much damage. A modern headmaster's natural desire to see all his boys through their schooltime to a satisfactory, if not triumphant, conclusion ought occasionally to take second place to the necessity of getting rid of one or two who are endangering the well-being of their immediate peers.

One source of harm in a boys' boarding community, homosexual behaviour, barely figures in accounts of Arnold's Rugby. This may be, as Professor Honey has suggested,[47] because in the first half of the nineteenth century, although there was a wide range of age (from 9 to 19) and of sexual maturity in a school, the schools seemed unconcerned over opportunities for homosexual temptation.[48] It was customary, for instance, for two or more boys to share a bed. Harper, Headmaster of Sherborne in the 1850s, writing to a new boy's parent, mentioned separate beds as a special advantage of the school. At Rugby before Arnold a single bed was charged as an extra on the bill, 4 guineas per annum, twice as expensive as sharing a bed with another boy. In the Rugby magazine of Arnold's day there is unabashed use of the word 'love' to describe boys' friendship. E. C. Mack, historian of public schools from 1780 onwards, cites the *Quarterly Journal of Education* of April–October 1835 for the first mention of sexual difficulities in the records.[49] Certainly homosexual vice did not become an issue until the second half of the century. In marked contrast to his attitude to lying, Arnold, according to Stanley, was sympathetic to boys found guilty of homosexual practices: 'At times on discovering cases of vice, he would, instead of treating them with contempt or extreme severity, tenderly allow the force of the temptation, and urge it upon them as a proof brought home to their own minds, how surely they must look for help out of themselves.'[50]

One reform that he introduced in School House which may well have reflected his concern over such misbehaviour was the introduction of a rule that boys should not visit each other's studies without good reason and the occupant's consent.[51] But apart from the general improvement of tone throughout the school, effected by his influence, and its transmission through the Sixth Form, he did not introduce many specific reforms. Indeed one disciplinary measure that he wished to introduce, solitary confinement as a punishment for certain offences, the Trustees refused to approve (Trustees' Order of 25 October 1831).[52] His usual approach was to modify existing policies that he disliked and thus reduce their ill effects. He continued, for example, to allow boys to fight each other, but insisted that they fought in the Close, rather than out of sight, and against an opponent of similar age and weight. Steeplechasing by older boys at nearby Dunchurch was stopped, the leading miscreant, as Thomas Hughes describes, tactfully but firmly dealt with. After the race was run, the Doctor summoned the Sixth-Former. 'I know all about the match you rode the other day,' he said. 'If I had taken any public notice of it, I must have expelled you . . . publicly. This would probably have ruined your career at Oxford, where you have just matriculated, and I hope will do well. But I have written to your father to tell him of your flagrant breach of discipline. And now let me warn you and your friends. I know what you are intending, and I will expel every boy who rides or is present, and will have the roads watched to get the names.' That race did not come off, or any other during Arnold's time.[53] But a few weeks later, when another steeplechase was held at Dunchurch, Arnold was shrewd enough to postpone the usual hour of the evening roll-call and to put Dunchurch in bounds for that day, so that all who wished could attend as spectators.[54]

He also made poaching and trespass much harder by putting out of bounds the houses where the boys hid their guns and dogs. The school's pack of beagles was put down, and the sport forbidden. Many public houses and the roads leading to them were also placed beyond bounds, and no alcohol was to be drunk anywhere in the school except beer at meals. The Sixth Form, however, were strongly opposed to this restriction and only the expulsion of one of their number for illegal drinking made them conform.[55] Even then they were most reluctant to stop other boys from drinking.

How far discipline really improved under Arnold is hard to discover. One Old Boy, W. E. Oswell, claimed that drinking was the vice of the school and that Arnold never managed to subdue it.[56] Another Old Boy, however, writing in 1838 towards the end of Arnold's time, said that he never knew the school more free from positive evil. By then roasting was unknown, tossing in blankets almost unknown, lying was scorned, drinking rare. Yet the picture painted in *Tom Brown's Schooldays* by Thomas Hughes, who was a boy in the school from 1833 to 1841 during Arnold's prime, or by George Melly, whose first two Rugby years coincided with Arnold's last two, is of a school where many of the traditional boarding vices—bullying, cruelty, cribbing (cheating at school work), deceit—were common. The Revd A. Orlebar, at Rugby from 1838 to 1843, reported that, though tossed himself in his first year, tossing had been given up before he left, and roasting *in a small way* (my italics) had replaced the dangerous sort of roasting described by Hughes. The custom of new boys singing indecent songs and the penalty, for resistance or breaking down, of having to drink drink a large mug of salt water, had been discontinued before 1850.[57] Moreover, Rugbeians who preceded Arnold, such as W. C. Lake, a pupil under both Wooll and Arnold, later Dean of Durham, and those who were boys under Arnold and Tait, such as Melly, do not suggest that for the ordinary schoolboy the characteristics of school life had altered substantially.[58] Stanley's account of the school's high moral tone was doubtless true for him since somehow he managed, for the most part, in spite of his saintly air, to avoid persecution and bullying.[59] He himself had moved into the Sixth Form with unusual speed and had thereafter developed a particularly close relationship with Arnold. For most boys, who left before the Sixth Form and therefore never came under Arnold's direct influence, and simply feared him from afar as Black Arnold, life was tough and often turbulent.

Undoubtedly many of his Sixth Form were deeply affected by Arnold. At Oxford, Rugbeians of that period were thought quite different from the ordinary run of public-school boy, thoughtful, manly-minded, conscious of duty. This manliness, not a masculine muscular ideal the converse of effeminacy, but an adult sense of duty and a mature determination to develop their moral character and intelligence so as to be Christian *men*, was the direct result of Arnold's teaching and preaching.[60] Yet that Arnold had a powerful effect on boys below the Sixth Form also, if not on their social behaviour (in the nature of things always resistant to radical reform), may be judged by Thomas Hughes's own address to the school on Quinquagesima Sunday, 8 February 1891, when he was a distinguished Old Boy and Queen's Counsel.[61] No boy, he claimed, could help being more or less under Thomas Arnold's influence, for the air of the whole place was full of it. In particular they had the feeling that they were in training for a big fight, were in fact already engaged in it, a fight which would last all their lives, and try them to the utmost—the fight of good with evil, of light and truth against darkness and lies, of Christ against the devil. They had, too, the conviction that if only they were true to their Captain, He was present with every one of them. Rugby was a missionary school. Finally, they were taught that there were subjects, such as the origin of evil, free will, God's omnipotence and omniscience, which lay beyond the range of the human intellect and before which they should be content to sit down patiently and quietly without attempting to find solutions.

Hughes went on to discuss objections that critics of Arnold's influence advanced: his masterfulness and habit of ignoring the other side of questions, which made his pupils dogmatists and weakened their hold on truth in later years when they learnt how complex serious problems were. He conceded that, though this criticism was untrue, Arnold's vigour and directness made some pupils readier to take sides and surer of their own judgement than young men should be.

'Is not training for the big fight', he concluded, '(to fight under Christ's banner against sin, the world, and the devil), the aim of all education in England worthy of the name since Alfred 1,000 years ago caused to be written up on the walls of his schools

> With all thy might
> Stand by the right
> And be thus strong
> Against the wrong'?

7

WRITING

'I claim a full right to use my own discretion in writing upon any subject I choose, provided I do not neglect my duties as master in order to find time for it. But those who know me will be aware that, to say nothing of my duty, my interest in the school far exceeds what I feel in any sort of composition of my own; and that neither here nor at Laleham, have I ever allowed my own writings to encroach upon the time, or on the spirits and vigour of mind and body, which I hold that my pupils have a paramount claim upon.'[1] Such was part of Arnold's reply to Dr Hawkins in May 1829, in which he refused to reprint his pamphlet on the Roman Catholic claims and stated that Rugby had not been and would not be harmed by the controversy over it.

Throughout his fourteen years as headmaster he wrote whenever he could find the time, driven on by an uncontrollable desire to set out on paper the thoughts that struggled within. 'I must write or die,' he said more than once.[2] He felt passionately that he had a message to deliver to his fellow-countrymen outside the school. Of eighteenth- and nineteenth-century headmasters only Dr Vicesimus Knox, the scholarly headmaster of Tonbridge from 1778 to 1812, whose *Collected Works* ran to seven volumes, was anywhere near as prolific. For an active headmaster Arnold's output was by any standard impressive. Not a year, from 1829 till his death in 1842, passed without some publication of his.

He wrote fast, almost without correction, in a plain conversational style, and readily admitted that through lack of imagination he could not achieve eloquence or mastery of language.[3] Even when writing on subjects of less immediate public concern, such as his *History of Rome*, he felt frustrated by his inability to express adequately the image of power and beauty that he saw there.[4]

He wrote very much as he thought, the expression of his ideas matching his mood of the moment. This was often as vehement as his speech; his impatience of the evils that he saw around him often gave his writing a polemical tone. Although he claimed to be willing to revise what he had written in order to accommodate legitimate criticism, his manuscripts show no evidence of such revision.[5] Usually he defended his views in retrospect as vigorously as when he had first set them down. Accused of arrogance in his pamphlet on the Roman Catholic claims, he replied that he did not consider it arrogance to assume that he knew more of a particular subject, which he had studied eagerly from childhood, than those who notoriously did not study it at all.[6]

Arnold's writings fall into three main groups, though all were spread across the years and interwoven in the business of his life: letters, sermons, and diaries, the most personal part of his output; articles, usually controversial, on educational issues and on current matters of Church and State; and his contributions to classical learning, particularly his massive commentary on Thucydides' *History of the Peloponnesian War* and a *History of Rome*. Right at the end of his life, on his appointment as Regius Professor of Modern History at Oxford, he gave eight lectures in January 1842, preceded in December by his Inaugural Lecture. He had also hoped to write in retirement, in addition, a full commentary on the New Testament and an extended treatise on Church and State.[7]

His letters, many of which are reprinted in whole or part in Stanley's *Life* and form the bulk of it, were written in the holidays or in the evenings at home during term time, or in class while the boys were busy with written work. He had many friends and evidently found relief in setting out his thoughts and plans to them, often repeating arguments that he had already published, as though they gained strength from repetition. His range is vast, as even the most cursory glance at the contents of Stanley's *Life* reveals, and the tone uniform, one of great moral earnestness and emphasis on practical considerations. There are few light touches, a sense of fun emerging occasionally, but no sense of humour or wit. The strength of his religious belief so permeated his personality that any form of frivolity found no place with him.[8]

Just as his huge correspondence formed an ever-present backcloth, so too his sermons, composed rapidly on a Sunday afternoon week after week (as we saw in Chapter 4), were an essential part of his busy life. As early as 1820 he admits to no longer writing just for enjoyment. 'I do nothing now in that way save sermons and letters.'[9]

That his sermons were highly effective we have seen already. He understood how to talk to boys. Early in his time at Rugby he made his purpose in preaching clear. 'I purpose . . . now . . . and . . . at some future times also, . . . to say something to you all about your own particular state and dangers; nor shall I care how plain and familiar is the language I use, as it is my wish to speak in such a manner that the youngest boy amongst you may understand, if he chooses to listen and attend.'[10] Though the expression of his thoughts was sometimes too complicated for younger boys, for the most part it was simple and direct, and easily understood.

His forays into journalism, however, were for the most part less effective and earned his friends' disapproval.[11] They feared that his work at Rugby would suffer and that his serious contributions to classical scholarship would be affected by his inability to refrain from meddling in politics. He felt strongly that 'bitterest of all griefs . . . , to see clearly and yet to be able to do nothing'.[12] As early as 1829 he had rushed to support a Bill on Catholic Emancipation. His pamphlet *The Christian Duty of Conceding the Claims of the Roman Catholics* (February 1829), though it pained several of his friends, received much acclaim. It was at least, as we have seen, on a subject that he had long thought about.[13] On the one hand, however, it was criticized by Liberals, who considered that the Roman Catholic Relief Bill was a political measure and could not be argued on religious grounds. Tories, on the other hand, agreed that it was a religious question on which the almost united authority of the English clergy should be decisive. Against both these points of view Arnold argued that it was a great national quest on of right and wrong which should be debated on Christian grounds, yet that the clergy were not the best judges since their training did not make them competent to pronounce on historical issues. The Relief Bill would, he suggested, be the best way of repairing the sin and mischief of the original conquest of Ireland, and was a right justly claimed by the Irish people.[14] The particular interest of this pamphlet lies in its being Arnold's first and most emphatic protest against the divorce of religion and politics. Perhaps encouraged by its reception, or more probably because he had the self-confidence to think he knew the cure for the country's ills, he founded in 1831 *The Englishman's Register*, in order to present his views on the society of his day, 'more to relieve his own conscience than with any sanguine hope of doing good'.[15] England was being endangered by the widening gulf between the educated and working classes. On the one hand the aristocrats opposed all efforts to raise the lower class, on the other those he called Jacobins aimed to reduce all classes to one low level. Both groups needed Christianizing.

The Englishman's Register ran for only a few weeks, cost him £200, and then folded. Disliked by the Tories for his Liberalism and scorned by the Reformers for his timidity, he had no solid core of supporters and was too concerned with moral rather than political issues. He had moreover neither the time nor the money nor the journalistic interest needed to make it a success. His patent sincerity, however, appealed so much to Mr Platt, the editor of the *Sheffield Courant*, that the latter reprinted some of his articles and persuaded him to write a series of thirteen letters on the chief causes of social distress in England.[16] The choice before the country, Arnold argued, lay between reform and revolution. People must have their physical needs satisfied before they are likely to look for general knowledge and the pleasures of the intellect.

He inveighed too against a *laissez-faire* economy in which working men were treated as pawns, not human beings.[17] It was no wonder that employers and employed grew ever further apart. These and other similarly radical contributions to the *Sheffield Courant* ceased with the passage of the Reform Bill in 1832, and it was not until 1837, towards the end of his life, that he began writing for a newspaper again. From that year until 1841 he published letters anonymously in the *Hertford Reformer* over the signature F. H. (Fox How). In these he continued to warn against the widening gap between the educated and the working classes, and Stanley records a letter from him to Carlyle (January 1840),[18] admittedly 'a perfect stranger', to canvass his support for a society that he was trying to form which would 'collect information [on] the condition of the poor throughout the Kingdom and . . . call public attention to it by every possible means'.[19]

Although he was aware that he lacked a journalist's skill in presenting his arguments forcefully and practically enough, and that friends and enemies were constantly criticizing him for not restricting his activities to Rugby, Arnold reckoned that his Radicalism would recruit more boys from Liberal families than he would lose.[20] In particular Theodore Hook, the editor of *John Bull*, campaigned relentlessly against him, warning parents that at Rugby 'boys are taught the language of heresy and nurtured up in the cradle of Radical reform'. The 'smirking, smiling' headmaster should stop 'scribbling to papers when he should be attending to business'.[21]

In March 1836, as was mentioned briefly in Chapter 3, Arnold had defended himself against such a charge to his old friend Coleridge, now a judge:

> . . . you express a wish that I would concentrate my energies upon the school, my own business. Why, you cannot surely think that . . . any man in England does so more than I do? I should feel it the greatest possible reproach, if I were conscious of doing otherwise. . . . I live for the school; that very pamphlet which I sent you was written almost entirely at Fox How, and my own employment here has been all of a kind to bear directly upon the school work; first, Thucydides, and now the Roman History, and subjects more or less connected with the Scriptures, or else my sermons. Undoubtedly, I do not wish my mind to feel less or to think less upon public matters; ere it does so, its powers must be paralysed; and I am sure that the more active my mind is, and the more it works upon great moral and political points, the better for the school; not of course, for the folly of proselytising the boys, but because education is a dynamical, not a mechanical process, and the more powerful and vigorous the mind of the teacher, the more clearly and readily he can grasp things, the better fitted he is to cultivate the mind of another.[22]

Coleridge was nevertheless right to remonstrate with his friend.[23] The numbers of boys at Rugby had been falling since 1834 and continued to fall until 1839. The continuous newspaper attacks of these years, especially of *John Bull* and the *Northampton Herald*, had their damaging effect. But Arnold was not dismayed.

Two other journalistic essays, both concerned with Church politics, also made him many enemies:[24] his pamphlet, *Principles of Church Reform*, published in 1833, and the anonymous article printed in April 1836 in the *Edinburgh Review*, entitled by the editor 'The Oxford Malignants', which was briefly discussed in Chapter 2 as precipitating a crisis with his governors. In the first of these, which is filled with criticism of creeds and sectarianism and urges a greater share by the laity in the government of the Church, a more popular constitution for it, and checks on episcopal powers, Arnold argued strongly against disestablishment. Establishment, he claimed, was a great national blessing, but it was based on too narrow a foundation and should be more comprehensive in its doctrines, constitution, and ritual. Although his theory of Church and State can be criticized for ignoring economics and allowing government too much power, the pamphlet was a major contribution to the discussion of reform and in part is still relevant.[25]

In the second essay Arnold attacked those at Oxford, especially Newman and Pusey, who had been campaiging against Dr Hampden, appointed Regius Professor of Divinity in the spring of 1836. Hampden's published opinions on the fallibility of Church authority and the comparative unimportance of dogma no doubt caused offence to Evangelicals and High-Churchmen chiefly because of his recent appointment to such an influential chair. (The present Bishop of Durham's experience in 1985 is not altogether dissimilar.) Of the many pamphlets occasioned by the controversy, Newman's elucidations of Dr Hampden's Theological Statements and Arnold's bitter reply in the *Edinburgh Review* were the two most powerful. For all his disagreement with the Tractarians, the latter was Arnold's only attack on them, but the severe way he wielded his pen, 'like a ferule', may be thought to have compensated for that. Newman and Pusey he called 'formalist, Judaizing fanatics who have ever been the peculiar disgrace of the Church of England', guilty not only of intellectual error but of moral wickedness also.[26]

During these particularly controversial years of 1834–5 when Arnold was deeply embroiled in public argument, he also published two long essays on educational topics, both anonymously, in the *Quarterly Journal of Education*, in Volume VII, No. XIV, on Rugby School and the teaching of classics, in Volume IX, No. XVIII on the Discipline of Public Schools, primarily a defence of fagging and corporal punishment. His views on discipline have been outlined earlier in Chapter 6, and his defence of the classics as an educational discipline is on traditional lines and was discussed in Chapter 5; neither bear further discussion here. Later, in 1839, he published a lecture which he had first delivered in 1838 to the Mechanics' Institute in Rugby, in order to promote the cause of adult education. Entitled 'On the Divisions and Mutual Relations of Knowledge', it is as dry as its title and, as his introduction suggests, wholly unremarkable.[27] Although written towards the end of his life, it conveys no new thinking.

Arnold's burning interest in the politics of Church and State of his day is doubtless one reason why he published comparatively little on educational topics and why, apart from his sermons, despite his belief that theology was more important than history and most needed his attention, he published so much less of the former. A long letter from Bonamy Price in Stanley's *Life*, setting out the principles of his exegesis, suggests other reasons: 'The prejudice of the clergy against him, the unripeness of England for a free and unfettered discussion of Scriptural exegesis, and the injury which he might be likely to do to his general usefulness.'[28] The Appendix to Volume II of the *Sermons* (the 'Essay on the Right Interpretation and Understanding of the Scriptures'), the Preface to Volume II, and Notes to Volume IV, are his only published work on the Bible. He himself, even in the last year of his life, and even though it was more misunderstood than any other of his writings, regarded the Essay as the most important thing he had ever written.[29] His knowledge of what the young wanted compelled him to it. The two considerations which he there set out as enabling a young man to find in the Old and New Testaments a consistent and all-sufficient guide for daily living, appropriately interpreted, still have relevance today; 'the commandments given to persons differently circumstanced from ourselves, while they are not directly binding on us so far as this difference extends, are yet a most valuable guide indirectly and by analogy; and that God's revelation to man, including in this term both communications of knowledge and directions for conduct, were adapted to his state at the several periods when they were successively made, so that actions may be even commanded at one period which, at another, men would have learnt to be evil, and which never therefore could be commanded to them'.[30] He was one of the first men in England to propound this theory of progressive revelation.[31]

From time to time in his correspondence we are given glimpses of his larger theological purpose, as for instance in May 1836 when he describes to the Archbishop of Dublin his plans for an edition of the three pastoral epistles (Timothy and Titus),[32] and again in November of the same year when he tells his old pupil W. C. Lake that he has translated almost half of St Paul's Epistle to the Thessalonians and is thinking of publishing his edition of these two books before that of the pastoral epistles.[33]

At the same time he was working on his Roman History, the first volume of which was published in 1838, whereas his editions of the Epistles, in spite of his feeling that they had a higher claim on him, never were. That he succeeded in publishing a massive three-volume edition of Thucydides' *History of the Peloponnesian War* and two complete volumes and a third incomplete of a *History of Rome* during his Rugby years, but no extensive theological work on the New Testament, requires explanation. Probably because he had to hand from 'the golden time'[34] of his Oxford years (between taking his degree and leaving the university for Laleham) so much more historical material, he would have found it easier, in the press of a headmaster's life, to put that into shape. Writing history was to him a relaxation and relief, a delightful παρεργον, whereas work on the New Testament was of high seriousness requiring that much more intellectual effort and uninterrupted time.[35]

In fact his historical writings were a leitmotif throughout his adult life,[36] covering three main stages: first, Laleham (August 1819–August 1827), where he wrote a short unpublished history of Greece, contributed a series of long articles to the *Encyclopaedia Metropolitana* on the Roman Republic and Empire (including essays on Hamilcar Barca, Hannibal, the Gracchi, Sulla, Julius Caesar, and the emperors Augustus and Trajan), and began editing Thucydides; secondly, his early years at Rugby (1827–34), where he published Volume I (covering Books I–III of Thucydides' *History*) in 1830, Volume II (Books IV and V) in 1832, and Volume III (Books VI–VIII), the last and best, in 1835; finally, Rugby 1835–42), when he resumed his Roman History, long put aside, publishing in 1838 the first volume ('Early History to the Burning of Rome by the Gauls'). Of the years 1833–5 Stanley tells us that 'what Fox How was to Rugby, that the Roman History was to the painful and conflicting thoughts roused by his writing on political and theological subjects'.[37] In 1840 came Volume II ('From the Gaulish Invasion to the End of the First Punic War'), and he was finding solace in writing Volume III ('From the End of the First to the End of the Second Punic War') during his last two years. As he wrote to the Revd J. Hearn in January 1841 from Fox How: '. . . I have had a very troublesome correspondence about school matters . . . my History is a great *diversion* from the cares about the school, and then the school work in its turn is a *diversion* from the thoughts about the History. Otherwise either would be rather overpowering . . .'[38] And in February 1842, on returning from his professorial lectures in Oxford,[39] he is eagerly back at work on the closing years of the Second Punic War. 'I thirst for Zama,' he said.[40] But death supervened before he could write his account of that decisive battle, and it was left to his friend the Revd J. C. Hare to publish the uncompleted third volume posthumously in 1843.

Although he wrote no full-length history of Greece, his particular sympathy always lay with Athens rather than Rome, and it is significant that his first main historical work was on his edition of Thucydides.[41] That this broke new ground in combining linguistic with historical and geographical notes, helped many to see the relevance of ancient history to modern politics,[42] and thus satisfied a real need, can be seen from its running to no fewer than ten editions. That Benjamin Jowett, classical scholar and famous Master of Balliol, should have commended it so enthusiastically is some measure of its worth. Although he had reservations about Arnold's linguistic and philological scholarship and criticized his fanciful comparisons of classical with biblical or modern events, he acclaimed his ability to translate with elegance and accuracy, his creation of interest in geography and archaeology, and his intelligent appreciation and good sense. Arnold's love of Thucydides inspired the love of him in others, and his commentary on Thucydides' *History* did much to make the geographical and historical elucidation of it fashionable.

His *History of Rome* also sold well. While it combined known facts rather than discovering the unknown, his composition and arrangement of these, his personal knowledge of the relevant geography, and his lively interest in military affairs gave the book a special interest. 'I have written the naval part of the First Punic War,' he writes in February 1840 to Chevalier Bunsen, 'with something of an Englishman's feeling.'[43] And in a letter from Fox How in January 1841 he told his brother-in-law, Trevenen Penrose, 'Though I have no good maps here, yet I am getting on with Hannibal's march from personal recollections of the country, which I think will give an air of reality to the narrative greater than it could have from maps.'[44]

Very much influenced in approach and content by the German scholar Niebuhr, who drew lessons from Republican Rome for Germany of his day, the *History* improves steadily as it moves from its account of the dim legendary origins of Rome to the portrayal of historical personages such as Scipio and Hannibal, and in spite of his outdated conception of history as a divine process with man morally accountable for his actions, his fluent colourful style carries the reader easily along.[45] As he expressed it to J. T. Coleridge in February 1837, 'I feel, too, that I have the love of history so strong in me, and that it has been working in me so many years, that I can write something which will be read, and which I trust will encourage the love of all things noble and just, and wise and holy.'[46] Again in September 1841 he repeats to the same correspondent a sentence from his Preface: 'If history has no truths to teach, its facts are little worth.' In December of the same year, in his inaugural lecture as Regius Professor of Modern History at Oxford, he dealt at greater length with the nature of history, which he defined as the biography of a nation, of a government, and with the value of the lessons that can be drawn from it. In the eight lectures he gave in Oxford during the Hilary term of 1842 he discussed further the relevance of the past to the present, and gave practical advice on how to study history.

The extent of his published works makes a modern headmaster feel inadequate. Yet such feelings can to some extent be assuaged by the consideration that the speed and ease of twentieth-century communications have enormously increased the day-to-day burdens of a headmaster's life. Without frequent visits of parents, actual and prospective, without business calls on the telephone, without the need to read a constant flow of ephemeral letters and papers (largely the consequence of the typewriter and the copier), emanating from educational agencies of all sorts, including the government, a nineteenth-century headmaster of what by modern standards was a small school of 300 boys could reasonably be expected to have had time, if he had the inclination, for scholarship. Nevertheless Arnold was the most prolific of his contemporaries among headmasters and wrote on a far wider variety of topics than any of them. Though little of this can be thought to have permanent merit, it is largely through his published sermons and letters that the strength and range of his views and of his personality can be directly gauged.

8

PARENTS

Of the five constituencies (pupils, parents, governors, former pupils, the wider community) to which a public-school headmaster is accountable, parents are, after the pupils, the most important.[1] For if the parents are dissatisfied, they will take their sons away. In Arnold's time, at least until the railways came, the remoteness of public schools from parents made it much easier for a school to ignore them. By contrast with today, when a boy or girl boarder can ring up his or her parents to complain and a parent can arrive by car the same or the following day if he wishes to follow up the complaint, a nineteenth-century headmaster need not have felt any immediate parental pressure. Dotheboys Hall would not last long in twentieth-century England.

There is little written evidence of Arnold's dealings with parents, not much correspondence and just a few notorious cases. As Stanley makes clear in his Preface,[2] he could not obtain most of the letters that Dr Arnold wrote to the parents of his pupils. If the letter to a parent holding Unitarian opinions, which *is* reproduced in Stanley's *Life*, is at all typical of Arnold's correspondence, it is a sad loss that most of it has not been published.

I had occasion to speak to your son this evening on the subject of the approaching confirmation; and, as I had understood that his friends were not members of the Established Church, my object was not so much to persuade him to be confirmed, as to avail myself of the opportunity thus afforded me to speak with him generally on the subject of his state as a Christian, and the peculiar temptations to which he was now peculiarly exposed, and the nature of that hope and faith which he would require as his best defence. But, on enquiring to what persuasion his friends belonged, I found that they were Unitarians. I felt myself therefore unable to proceed, because, as nothing would be more repugnant to my notions of fair dealing, than to avail myself indirectly of my opportunities of influencing a boy's mind contrary to the religious belief of his parents, without giving them the fullest notice, so, on the other hand, when the differences of belief are so great and so many, I feel that I could not at all enter into the subject, without enforcing principles wholly contrary to those in which your son has been brought up. This difficulty will increase with every half-year that he remains at the school, as he will be gradually coming more and more under my immediate care; and I can neither suffer any of those boys with whom I am more immediately connected, to be left without religious instruction, nor can I give it in his case, without unavoidably imparting views, wholly different from those entertained by the persons whom he is naturally most disposed to love and honour. Under the circumstances, I think it fair to state to you, what line I shall feel bound to follow, after the knowledge which I have gained of your son's religious belief. In everything I should say to him on the subject, I should use every possible pains and delicacy to avoid hurting his feelings with regard to his relations; but at the same time, I cannot avoid labouring to impress on him, what is my belief on the most valuable truths in Christianity, and which, I fear, must be sadly at variance with the tenets in which he has been brought up. I should not do this controversially, and in the case of any other form of dissent from the Establishment, I would avoid dwelling on the differences between us, because I could teach all that I conceive to be essential in Christianity, without at all touching upon them. But in this instance, it is impossible to avoid interfering with the very points most at issue. I have a very good opinion of your son, both as to his conduct and his abilities, and I should be very sorry to lose him from the school. I think, also, that any one who knows me, would give you ample assurance that I have not the slightest feeling against Dissenters as such, or any desire, but rather very much the contrary, to make this school exclusive. My difficulty with your son is not one which I feel as a Churchman, but as a Christian; and goes only on this simple principle, that I feel bound to teach the essentials of Christianity to all those committed to my care—and with these the tenets of the Unitarians alone, among all the Dissenters in the kingdom, are in my judgment irreconcilable. I trust that you will forgive me for having troubled you thus at length on this subject.[3]

In this he shows an honesty, sensitivity, and determination that are wholly characteristic and may be taken as typical of his attitude to parents, at least those with whom he had no quarrel. His high regard for the influence of home and his grave reservations about the value of boarding-school alike combined to make him anxious to keep closely in touch with the parents of his charges.[4] Not only, as we saw in Chapter 5, did he introduce the practice of writing reports regularly on the progress of boys in his House, but he preached to the school more than once on the importance of not neglecting their homes and families, and constantly advocated the superior benefits of being a day boy at a public school in reaping the advantages of home as well as school without the drawbacks of the latter.[5] 'I was for some years', wrote an anonymous Old Rugbeian, quoted by Selfe, 'in the School House and was not either intellectually or by industrious study such a pupil as to attract the special attention of his master, but I found amongst my father's papers letters from Dr Arnold in which year after year he discussed my progress and conduct up to the time of my leaving.'[6] We have evidence also of Arnold writing to Stanley's father inviting him over to Rugby to hear his son deliver his Prize Essay in public (at the annual Speech Day),[7] and a similar invitation survives in a final report by Dr Arnold to A. H. Clough's uncle.

Dr Thomas Arnold to Alfred B. Clough. Rugby, October 19th 1837.

My dear Sir,

I did not write to you when your nephew left us, but I must take the opportunity of one of our men's going to Oxford tomorrow, to send you these few lines. I cannot resist my desire of congratulating you most heartily on the delightful close of your nephew's long career at Rugby, where he has passed eight years without a fault, so far as the school is concerned, where he has gone on ripening gradually in all excellence intellectual and spiritual, and from whence he was now gone to Oxford, not only full of honours, but carrying with him the respect and love of all whom he has left behind, and regarded by myself, I may truly say, with an affection and interest hardly less than I should feel for my own son. I only hope, and indeed nothing doubt, that you will have the same pleasure in watching his career at Oxford that I have long had in watching it at Rugby.

Our Speeches have been transferred from Easter to the third week in June, which I hope will suit our Oxford friends as well. And although your personal connection with Rugby is at an end, yet I hope that we shall have the pleasure of seeing you here from time to time amongst us, as we had before your nephew left us.[8]

Copies also exist of some early circular letters, in his own hand, which he sent to parents, a short one dated 6 January 1830 telling them of a smallpox outbreak in Rugby and urging vaccination of their sons, and another dated 17 April 1830 asking for their help in checking some undesirable practices connected with the feasts given by boys on being promoted from one form to another. Similar in style and intent to many a letter written by modern headmasters to their pupils' parents, it shows good sense and tact:

Having received from several quarters complaints of the expense incurred by the boys in the feasts which they have been accustomed to give on their promotion from one form to another;—and being aware that they are in the habit of applying regularly to their friends for money for this purpose, I have thought it best to write this circular letter, to request your cooperation in correcting the evils to which the practice in question has given occasion.

It is so desirable to deprive boys of all excuse for clandestine proceedings, that I have thought it better to put the practice under regulations than to forbid it altogether; and I am inclined to think that if the expense is reduced within proper limits, the mischief of the thing will be removed.

I venture to request therefore, that you will never on any consideration allow your boy more than fifteen shillings for one of these feasts; and this only on his promotion from the Remove or Shell to the Fifth Form:—that on his promotion from the Fourth to the Remove the sum given should never exceed ten shillings; and that on his promotion from the Third to the Fourth, it should never exceed eight. I shall desire that notice may always be given to the master of the boarding house; of the time when these feasts are to take place; in order that nothing improper, and particularly no wine or spirituous liquors, may be introduced at them.

May I also earnestly request, that you will never send your boy any game, or other meat unless previously ordered, as we have found that when the boys receive game, it leads to a great deal of cooking, and I fear, in some instances, to drinking?

No feasts have been given on the promotion of boys from the Fifth Form to the Sixth, or from the Second Form to the Third and I shall strictly prevent the practice from extending to these occasions.

I have the honour to be, Sir,
Your very obedt humble Servt
T. Arnold[9]

A letter of 1835 written to the mother of Henry Hatch, one of his prefects, shows similar sensitivity and practical sense.[10] Hatch had fallen ill just as he was preparing for the entrance examination to Oxford, in which he hoped to gain an Exhibition that would enable him to afford a university education, for his parents were not wealthy enough to pay their son's fees. Arnold persuaded his assistant masters to raise enough money privately to give the boy some £40 or so a year for four years so that he had no need to sit the entrance examination. 'The masters', he wrote to Mrs Hatch, 'feel so strongly his remarkably good conduct ever since he has been at Rugby that they propose to offer him from themselves an Exhibition for four years. . . . Our object in doing this was, amongst others, to prevent him working at the examination which, we are sure, would, in his present state of health, be very injurious to him.'

Yet though he was clearly anxious to keep in close touch with parents about their sons and was sensitive to their needs, he was adamant that parents had no right to keep their sons at school against its interests, and his attitude to parents who crossed him was on occasions ruthless and inexcusable.

The case of the boy Marshall illustrates this.[11] On Friday, 13 November 1835 Nicholas Marshall, a boy in the Lower Fifth in Anstey's House, having impetuously defied a prefect, was told to present himself for punishment in Hall after dinner. There he found three prefects who had evidently conjectured that, being physically strong, he might resist a caning. Their expectations were confirmed. As soon as he began to be beaten, he seized the cane and broke it in half. The affair became a brawl, with one of the three prefects trying to hit the younger boy with a knotted blackthorn stick while the other two held him. Marshall managed to grab the stick and escape. But his triumph did not last long. He was summoned by the headmaster on the prefects' complaint and, without being given any chance to defend his conduct, summarily expelled. Arnold always backed his prefects. Although it was late in the day and darkness had fallen, the boy was forthwith dispatched in a chaise to his home at Iffley, some fifty miles distant in Oxfordshire.

The boy's father was deeply upset, incensed not only by the expulsion, which seemed excessive punishment, but also by the unfeeling way it had been carried out. His letter of complaint to Arnold was ignored, so he decided to take his other son away from Rugby also. Arnold still refusing to answer his letters, he thought to visit the school and confront the headmaster in person. Unwisely he made no appointment and arrived to find Arnold in no mood for sensible discussion. For he had just finished dealing with another angry parent who had been complaining of a similar example of prefectorial bullying. Arnold turned Marshall's father away without even a hearing. Infuriated by the discourtesy and the waste of a long journey, the father appealed to the Trustees. He was told that he could make his case at their next routine meeting in July. Before then the Trustees had held a special meeting, in March, and put on record their 'entire satisfaction with Dr Arnold's conduct in the management of the school'.[12] In July Marshall's father was informed that having expressed confidence in their headmaster in

March they regarded the affair as closed. He was rightly indignant at the gross injustice that he and his son had suffered.

The Wratislaw saga, which was much more complex and spread over many years, sheds, if anything, a still more unpleasant light on Arnold's treatment of parents.

At the start of Arnold's headmastership William Ferdinand Wratislaw, a local solicitor, who shared the headmaster's radical sympathies, was a friend and one of his very few effective supporters in the town. In 1830, for example, probably at Arnold's instance, he complained to the Directors of the London and Birmingham Railway about the proposed line of the track, as being too close to the school on its south side—to some effect, because in 1831 the route was altered to where it runs today, well clear to the north. That he was still supporting him in 1835 is clear from his taking Arnold's side when he urged that the *Northampton Herald* should be banned from the town reading room because of its scurrilous attacks on the headmaster. But by the summer of 1836 friendship had changed to enmity, and Wratislaw had removed the eldest of his five sons, Albert, from the school in protest over what he regarded as Arnold's failure to recognize the rights of the local townspeople in the education of their sons.

Laurence Sheriff, the school's founder in 1567, had aimed to establish a grammar school under a Master of Arts, which should provide a free education in the classics to the boys chiefly of Rugby and Brownsover 'and next for such as bee of other places thereunto adjoining'. Gradually, however, as the years passed, fee-paying pupils came to be admitted as boarders because there were too few local boys to make a viable school, so by 1800 the school catered primarily for the needs of the 'gentry', with pupils drawn from all over Britain and a few even from overseas.[13] The few local boys who came from upper-class or professional families were admitted as Foundationers, that is free Scholars on the Laurence Sheriff Foundation. In theory, this privilege was open to all the sons of those who had resided for two years or more in Rugby, or in Warwickshire within ten miles, or in Leicestershire or Northamptonshire within five miles, but few took advantage of it, fewer indeed than three middle-class pupils on average being admitted each year. Lower-class children saw the inside of the school only as servants. So at the start of the nineteenth century the Founder's design had been frustrated. From time to time the Trustees of the school were challenged on the position. A Mr Stratford took them to court before the Lord Chancellor in 1808, arguing that the surplus income from the endowment should be spent for the benefit of the boys in the Rugby neighbourhood. The Trustees, however, who had accumulated over £40,000 and spent less than half of the endowment income of almost £3,500 each year, wanted to build a new and larger school.[14] They won their case, the Founder's will was overruled, and Rugby was set to be a national public school.[15]

In February 1836 Wratislaw made another attempt to secure free education, in accordance with the Founder's wish, for local boys. Incidental expenses were now so great that only the richest of middle-class families could afford to send their sons as Foundationers, and Wratislaw argued that the unspent balance of income each year should be put to reducing the educational costs of the poorer boys. The Trustees responded by agreeing to cancel all such expenses, but there was still the problem for boys of qualifying for promotion from the Lower to the Upper School. The age of transfer was as today 12 or 13, the Lower School being essentially a preparatory department which taught classics to boys from the age of 7 or 8. Boys had to be competent in Latin to earn promotion, so that teaching in the Lower School had to be efficient if they were not to languish indefinitely there. Properly taught, a boy, entering at 7 or 8, could move steadily through to the Upper School.

Under Wooll there had been problems in the Lower School: numbers had declined sharply from 187 to 23 in 1828.[16] On his arrival, Arnold was at first convinced by Wratislaw of the desirability of strengthening the Lower School. He probably needed little persuasion, for one of his first tasks was clearly to raise the numbers of the school as a whole. So the Lower School grew quickly in size: 47 boys in 1829, 94 in 1830, 112 in 1834, the peak year. By 1830 an extra form was needed, and one of Arnold's best schoolmasters, Bonamy Price, had been placed in charge of it. So Wratislaw and other local parents thought that they could look forward to a good education for their children from 7 or 8 upwards with every prospect of their being promoted in due course to the Upper School.

But their expectations were short-lived. For by 1838 there was once more only a rump in the Lower School, a mere 38 pupils, and local boys were no longer being given adequate preparation for the Upper School. At some point in the 1830s Arnold had come to the conclusion that boys should not enter a public school before the age of 12, and had begun to run the Lower School numbers down accordingly.

Of Wratislaw's five sons, Albert, who had entered the Lower School in 1829, had made good progress. The next two, Charles and William, who both joined the bottom form in 1834, did not. Nor were other boys in the Lower School doing well. Teaching was ineffective. Extra tuition out of school was necessary if they were to qualify for the Upper School. This was costly and made a boy's working day too long. Besides, it was wholly contrary to the spirit of the Foundation.

In August 1836, after a quarrel with Arnold, Wratislaw, as we saw earlier, withdrew Albert. What caused the dispute is not clear, but it is likely to have been, at least partly, due to Wratislaw's dissatisfaction with Arnold's arrangements for the Lower School. Strangely perhaps, Charles and William stayed on through 1836 and 1837, and with special coaching out of school made progress.

The crunch came in 1838. By then Wratislaw's fourth son was 7 and would soon be ready for school, to be followed two years later by the last of the family, Henry. But by then, too, Arnold had discontinued the first two forms of the Lower School, so that Wratislaw had either to engage a private tutor for the two boys to qualify them for entry to the Third Form or do battle in the courts.

He chose the latter course: with the help of H. W. S. Gibb, another local citizen, who had nine sons, he took a petition to the Chancery Court. They had three complaints: first, that Exhibitions (that is what today would be called School Leaving Exhibitions to help a boy financially through university) were awarded to local and non-local boys equally; secondly, that children whose parents had not been resident locally for two years were excluded from the school; and thirdly, that young boys were discouraged from entering the school, so that boys entitled to benefit from it were obliged from an early age to have a prior or preparatory education, to fit them for education in the school as now conducted.

On the first complaint, Lord Langdale, Master of the Rolls, who heard the case, concluded that he could not decide against Lord Eldon who in 1806 had ruled that Exhibitions might be awarded to Scholars not on the Foundation, and since 1806 there had been no change in circumstances such as to justify his overruling the earlier judgement.

Between 1780 and 1805, on average a quarter of the Scholars taught were Foundationers, and of the 63 boys elected to Exhibitions 21 were Foundationers, and 42 not on the Foundation. Thus Foundationers had fared proportionately better than boys from outside Rugby.

The second complaint was even less convincing. In 1830 the Trustees had resolved that their express sanction must be obtained at their annual meeting before any boy be admitted on the Foundation whose parents or guardians had not been resident for two years within the limits of the Foundation. The effect of this was not to exclude boys for longer than from one annual July meeting to the next, and it was a reasonable safeguard against too many outsiders taking up residence in Rugby in order to get a good education for their sons on the cheap. The restriction in no way affected boys who were members of long-standing local families. Lord Langdale ruled that, since there was no instance of inconvenience or of any individual being excluded from the school, no order from him was required or would indeed be proper. The matter could safely be left to the Trustees.

The third complaint, however, had substance. Young boys were being discouraged from entry to the school, and thus the interests of the potential Foundationers were prejudiced. While under Dr Arnold the school had greatly flourished, numbers rising from 111 in 1827 to 274 in 1838, the Lower School numbers had not risen proportionately, being 25 in 1827 and only 38 in 1838.

Counsel for Wratislaw and Gibb argued that this decline was due to Arnold's deliberate policy. As early as 1831 he planned to discontinue the First and Second Forms, for in that year he had put in charge of the First Form the writing master, a Mr Sale, who was not a classicist and had no knowledge of Latin. Not only did he have more than enough work as writing master, but he had been appointed to succeed James Prince Lee, a far more knowledgeable and effective teacher. By 1836 the First Form had 4 members; in 1837 it no longer existed.

The history of the Second Form was equally to Arnold's discredit. In 1832 he appointed a Swiss, Louis Pons, as its form master. Though a good Latinist, Pons pronounced the language in the Continental manner so that the boys had great difficulty in understanding him. Moreover he was often absent through ill health and even when present could not control the boys. Numbers had fallen from 29 in 1832, to 6 in 1837. The form was then closed. So in 1838 the school's two bottom forms, the first two rungs on the ladder which led to the Upper School, were no more.

Arnold's defence was feeble and disingenuous. The two teachers, Sale and Pons, he claimed, were adequate and he himself regularly examined the forms and saw nothing amiss. That neither Sale nor Pons was called in evidence suggests that the Trustees knew that the school's case was weak.[17]

Arnold was also criticized for positively discouraging local parents from sending their sons to the school. Though he denied that he had refused admission to any boy who could read English and was entitled to be a Foundationer, he certainly seems to have done nothing to encourage members of the Rugby community to enter their sons.[18] Whether, as T. W. Bamford suggests, this was due to his lack of sympathy for the very young or, as D. Newsome argues, due to his desire to preserve the school's national character and prevent its being swamped by local children claiming to benefit from Laurence Sheriff's Foundation, is not clear.[19] Whatever his motive, Arnold's behaviour appeared ruthless and unsympathetic.

The case was heard over three days in January 1838 and in May Lord Langdale gave his judgement. He did not think it 'desirable to discourage the entrance of boys under 12', and considered that such a course of proceedings would not be beneficial to the objects of the charity. He was against 'ordering forms to be established before there are boys to be instructed upon them' but 'provision ought to be made for the instruction in the school of young boys who can read *English* and are capable of being instructed in the first elements of grammar'.[20]

But since the Trustees prudently let it be known that they wished to give effect to this judgement, the court made no order on the petition. The Trustees were nevertheless required to pay the substantial costs of the case. Yet though this indicated that the school had had the worst of the argument, Arnold had won the day. He had been given no specific instructions; he was not required to restore the First and Second Forms. While he clearly felt bound to admit those Gibb and Wratislaw sons who had not yet entered the school, he had no intention of going out of his way to promote the entry of boys under 12 who knew English but no Latin. He had always prided himself on being independent of his governors, so he had no need to take their wishes too seriously.

The episode reveals a level of deceit and ruthlessness that is plainly discreditable. To have taken younger boys, and to continue taking them, into such a badly taught Lower School, knowing that they would be most unlikely to earn promotion into the Upper School unless they had private tuition outside, was taking them on false pretences. It is curious that the only reference to the affair in Stanley's *Life*, a letter of 8 May 1838 from Arnold to Mr Justice Coleridge, points to Arnold's anxiety on the score of financial impropriety, which to the modern observer misses the point.

But despite such instances of gross insensitivity, not to say ruthlessness, in his dealings with a few parents and despite the criticisms which his participation in public controversies provoked, it cannot be doubted that in the main he reconciled upper-middle-class parents to the public schools. The increase in numbers at Rugby and other similar schools, and the foundation of new public schools shortly after his death, alike confirm this.

9

INFLUENCE

Dean Lake's opinion that Arnold's influence did not materially change the character of school life for the ordinary boy we saw confirmed in Chapter 6 by *Tom Brown's Schooldays* and George Melly's *School Experiences of a Fag*.[1] Both describe an essentially unreformed public school, with much characteristic schoolboy 'crime'. Poaching, illegal drinking, smoking, fighting, bullying, cruelty, untrustworthy prefects—all continued throughout Arnold's headmastership, though no doubt less so at its end than at its start. Arnold himself recognized this: in his last sermon he said '. . . there are still existing certain influences for evil in our society itself of the same sort as formerly . . .'.[2] Carlyle, on the strength of a week's visit near the end of Arnold's time, called the school 'a temple of industrious peace', but he was staying on the private side of School House and looking at the school from the outside. Most headmasters are adept at keeping their public and private lives separate, at preventing the intrusion into their homes of school problems and crises. Rugby remained, in the words of an Old Boy, the Revd Bulkely O. Jones, a 'rough and tumble' sort of place in the 1830s and 1840s.[3] Arnold would not have demurred: in a letter of 1840 he wrote: 'I have many delightful proofs that those who have been here have found at any rate no such evil as to prevent their serving God in after life: and some, I trust, have derived good from Rugby. But the evil is great and abounding, I well know; and it is very fearful to think that it may to some be irreparable ruin.'[4]

Day-to-day school life for many boys, then, was not radically improved by Arnold, nor, as we saw in Chapter 5, was he the author of any major educational reforms. He simply introduced to Rugby curricular developments that had already been introduced elsewhere.

He added no new buildings except the tower room over the front gate, built in 1829, to which he moved the school library and in which he taught the Sixth; by way of contrast, Edward Thring, headmaster of Uppingham a few years after Arnold's death (1853–87), built a concert hall and gymnasium. Arnold was not interested in art, music, or physical education. Socially, his replacement of dames, who were not members of the teaching staff, by housemasters in the boarding-houses was his most significant reform, although, as noted in Chapter 2, this development occurred at other schools also at this time. Pastoral care and House discipline must have improved for most boys as a consequence, but living conditions remained much as before.

The prefect system, too, at its best undoubtedly ameliorated the worst excesses of boarding-school life and improved the tone of the school in some degree, but at a price. The moral and religious pressure placed on boys in the Sixth Form was too much for some. A. H. Clough, at school one of Arnold's favourite pupils, who while a boy supported his headmaster's policy with fervent admiration, in later life expressed his reservations in the epilogue to his long poem *Dipsychus*, an imaginary conversation with his uncle, educated at a public school before Arnold. Discussing schools with his nephew, the uncle says:

'. . . consciences are often much too tender in your generation—schoolboys' consciences too! As my old friend the Canon says of the Westminster students, "they're all so pious". It's all Arnold's doing; he spoilt the public schools. . . . Not that I mean that the old schools were perfect, any more than we old boys that were there. But whatever else they were or did, they certainly were in harmony with the world, and they certainly did not disqualify the country's youth for after-life and the Country's service. . . . "Young men must be young men," as the worthy head of your College said to me (touching a case of rustication). "My dear sir," said I, "I only wish to heaven that they would be; but as for my own nephews, they seem to be a sort of hobbadi-hoy cherub, too big to be innocent, and too simple for anything else. They're full of the notion of the world being so wicked, and of their taking a higher line, as they call it. I only fear they'll never take any at all." . . . [Arnold] used to attack offences, not as offences—the right view—against discipline, but as sin, heinous guilt, I don't know what else beside! Why didn't he flog them and hold his tongue? Flog them he did, but why preach?' [The nephew replies:] 'If he did err in this way, sir . . . I ascribe it to the spirit of the time. The real cause of the evil you complain of . . . was . . . the religious movement of the last century, beginning with Wesleyanism and culminating at last in Puseyism. This over-excitation of the religious sense, resulting in this irrational, almost animal irritability of conscience, was in many ways as foreign to Arnold as it is proper to ——' [the uncle interrupts].[5]

To those who responded to his pressure Arnold gave so much responsibility that they became self-important prigs, overfull of their headmaster's liberal ideals. Clough admitted later that he had less boyish enjoyment of any kind while at school than nine-tenths of his peers. Lake, too, criticized Arnold for pressing his boys, intellectually and physically, to become men before their time.[6] C. H. Pearson, who joined the school a year after Arnold died, was similarly critical: 'Arnold's pupils . . . were taught to be always feeling their moral muscles, always careful about their schoolfellows' morality. . . . The precepts were more weighty than boys could assimilate without incessant pretentiousness . . .'[7] Life was too earnest and lacked all humour: what Arnold called 'awful wickedness' was often really just mere schoolboy fun.[8]

Though these criticisms have some justification, though there were no particularly original or striking reforms of curriculum, constitution, administration, or everyday life, the fact remains that Arnold restored confidence in the public schools.[9] His earnest, high-minded approach appealed to many parents, of both the upper and the new middle class.[10] Thus the children of the old and new ruling groups were intermingled. Professedly liberal in outlook, as we saw in Chapter 3, he was fundamentally conservative in action, and his religious enthusiasm fitted well with the religious revival then current. His unwavering determination to send out Christian men into the world matched the mood of the well-to-do classes. His weekly sermons in chapel, another innovation of his, were all part of this desire to Christianize society. Despite its loss of popularity and decline in numbers in the mid-thirties at the height of his controversies, the school by his last years was again full and his reputation assured.

It was not, however, yet a great reputation, and the report of his death in *The Times* of 16 June 1842 was brief,[11] in marked contrast with its description over fifty years later (17 July 1896) of the Westminster Abbey ceremony at which a marble bust of Arnold was unveiled there by an Old Rugbeian, Dean Bradley.[12] Why and how did his fame grow so great? Is it justified?

The loyalty of his staff and the devotion of a number of his pupils are the main reasons for its growth, expressed in particular in two books, A. P. Stanley's *Life* and Thomas Hughes's *Tom Brown's Schooldays*.

Stanley joined the school in January 1829 aged 13, only a few months after Arnold himself, and remained there until 1834.[13] Well taught and exceptionally intelligent, he was promoted so rapidly through the school's lower forms that in six months he had reached the Fifth Form and was thereafter exempt from fagging, not that during those few months he fagged more than once, being usually excused by the prefects. Despite his slight stature and feminine appearance, despite his shyness and timidity, he was scarcely ever teased, his nickname Nancy being soon forgotten.[14] He claimed to have been much bullied in his first House but this phase did not last long. His ability to help his fellow-pupils with their schoolwork compensated fully for his not taking part in games, and such were his charm and vivacity when he was accosted that soon potential bullies left him alone and some boys voluntarily fagged for him even before he was in the Sixth Form. Somehow he never seemed to his contemporaries to be a normal boy, and though respected he was never really popular. On one occasion indeed he was stoned through his study window because he was reading.[15] Gradually this precocious scholar developed a strong admiration for, not to say love of, Arnold, to whom he was a star pupil, and in 1834, when head of his House, he, with Lake and Vaughan, two other favourites of the Doctor, suppressed an incipient rebellion. At Oxford later, he maintained his close friendship with his former headmaster, whom he regarded as his 'idol and oracle, both in one',[16] and at the latter's death in 1842 he was invited by Mrs Arnold to write a memoir of her husband. He spent as much time in the next two years on this enterprise as he could spare from his college duties and when what had turned into a full-length biography was published in May 1844, it was an immediate success. As a letter from the Dean of Salisbury, the Very Revd G. D. Boyle, later put it: '. . . from the moment that Dean Stanley's admirable *Life* appeared, Arnold's influence, hitherto confined to his own pupils, became a moving force in English school life'.[17]

The *Life*, the portrait of the hero schoolmaster by his hero pupil, was indeed so successful that all biographers and students of Arnold's life have been heavily reliant on it since.[18] The volume and range of his correspondence to his friends there recorded and the warmth of Stanley's enthusiasm for his subject convey an unforgettable impression of Arnold's powerful and committed personality. The posthumous tribute of a contemporary headmaster, Dr Moberly, printed by Stanley as a coda to his own account of school life at Rugby, which was briefly mentioned earlier (in Chapter 3), deserves to be set out in full as evidence of Arnold's influence on his boys.

'Possibly,' he writes, after describing his own recollections as a schoolboy,

> other schools may have been less deep in these delinquencies than Winchester; I believe that in many respects they were. But I did not find, on going to the University, that I was under disadvantages as compared with those who came from other places; on the contrary, the tone of young men at the University, whether they came from Winchester, Eton, Rugby, Harrow, or wherever else, was universally irreligious. A religious undergraduate was very rare, very much laughed at when he appeared; and I think I may confidently say, hardly to be found among public school men; or, if this be too strongly said, hardly to be found except in cases where private and domestic training, or good dispositions, had prevailed over the school habits and tendencies. A most singular and striking change has come upon our public schools—a change too great for any person to appreciate adequately, who has not known them in both these times. This change is undoubtedly part of a general improvement of our generation in respect of piety and reverence, but I am sure that to Dr Arnold's personal simplicity of purpose, strength of character, power of influence, and piety, which none who ever came near him could mistake or question, the carrying of this improvement into our schools is mainly attributable. He was the first. It soon began to be matter of observation to us in the University, that his pupils brought quite a different character with them to Oxford than that which we knew elsewhere. I do not speak of opinions; but his pupils were thoughtful, manly-minded, conscious of duty and obligation, when they first came to college; we regretted, indeed, that they were often deeply imbued with principles which we disapproved, but we cordially acknowledged the immense improvement in their characters in respect of morality and personal piety, and looked on Dr Arnold as exercising an influence for good, which (for how many years I know not) had been absolutely unknown to our public schools.
>
> I knew personally but little of him. You remember the first occasion on which I ever had the pleasure of seeing him: but I have always felt and acknowledged that I owe more to a few casual remarks of his in respect of the government of a public school, than to any advice or example of any other person. If there be improvement in the important points, of which I have been speaking at Winchester, (and from the bottom of my heart I testify with great thankfulness that the improvement is real and great,) I do declare, in justice that his example encouraged me to hope that it might be effected, and his hints suggested to me the way of effecting it.
>
> I fear that the reply, which I have been able to make to your question,

will hardly be so satisfactory as you expected, as it proceeds so entirely upon my own observations and inferences. At the same time I have had, perhaps, unusual opportunity for forming an opinion, having been six years at a public school at the time of their being at the lowest,—having then mingled with young men from other schools at the University, having had many pupils from different schools, and among them several of Dr Arnold's most distinguished ones; and at last, having had near eight years' experience, as the master of a school, which had undergone, in great measure, the very alteration which I have been speaking of. Moreover, I have often said the very things, which I have here written, in the hearing of men of all sorts, and have never found anybody disposed to contradict them.

Believe me, my dear Stanley,
Yours most faithfully,
George Moberly.[19]

But this generous testimonial was strongly criticized as an unfair overstatement by Charles Wordsworth, the poet's nephew and second master under Moberly, who considered that their reforms at Winchester had in no way been inspired by Arnold.

I think it only right to qualify the impression which Moberly's letter is calculated to convey, in simple justice to other reformers, and not least to Moberly himself. The truth is, there was a general awakening which in many instances, as with us at Winchester, *partook decidedly of a church character*, such as Arnold's teaching and example, however excellent in their way, had little or no tendency to create.[20]

Indirect confirmation that Arnold's reputation came after his death comes from two other sources also. Bulwer Lytton, writing on the education of England and the English in 1833, had similar aims for public schools to Arnold's, but neither knew of the other.[21] A letter from Samuel Butler, the headmaster of Shrewsbury, who presided over its renaissance from 1798 to 1836, shows clearly that schools at this time could be unaffected by educational developments in other parts of England. Writing in 1835 to a favourite pupil, Benjamin Hall Kennedy, the author of the well-known Latin Grammar who was himself later to be a distinguished headmaster of Shrewsbury, he said, 'I don't know what you mean by Arnold's reform of Rugby. You are probably better informed than I am, and allude to something with which I am unacquainted, but I can only say that I never heard of such an act. I know he increased the numbers very much, and I hear that they are now considerably on the decline again, but I do not know anything more.'[22] This view finds an echo in his grandson's biography, published in 1896: 'Dr Arnold unquestionably made a deep impression on those boys who were brought into close communication with himself but I cannot find that his (Dr Arnold's) influence over the school survived longer than that of any subsequent headmaster, while upon other schools, so far as I have been able to ascertain, he produced—I believe it is not too much to say—no effect whatever.'[23] Grandfilial loyalty and a certain natural perversity of nature must be held responsible for this atypical reaction. But it does represent in an extreme form that strain of opinion which from the first was critical of Arnold and considered his reputation exaggerated.

If Stanley's veneration of Arnold verged on the idolatrous[24] and if the effect of his biography on the public can be attributed to the extent of his devotion and of his literary skill in expressing it, he was nevertheless far from being the only admirer of the Doctor. W. C. Lake, a more ordinary Rugbeian than Stanley, who yet claimed to have known Arnold far more intimately, praised him almost as fulsomely in his review of Stanley's *Life* in the *Quarterly Review* of October 1844.[25] His portrayal, though more critical, confirms Arnold's essential characteristics as Stanley describes them.

Yet Lake saw clearly what damage Arnold's pressure on sensitive pupils could do.[26] A. H. Clough never fulfilled his school promise, but despite Lytton Strachey's sneering reference to him reduced in his last days to doing menial work for Florence Nightingale, this failure can hardly be regarded as solely Arnold's responsibility.[27] Judging a headmaster's success by his pupils gives him too much credit if they succeed in later life and too little if they do not. The genetic factor, the early home environment, and the influence of peers make a far more powerful combination for good or ill than any one headmaster, whether he be an Arnold or not. What is to the point here is that boys as different as Stanley, Lake, Clough, Hughes, and many more, not only felt his influence so strongly during their schooldays and, in some cases, for many years after, but acted on it as well and in different ways. Divergent though their achievements were, they all had one characteristic in common, moral idealism.[28] C. J. Vaughan, for example, the third of the trio of boys so influential at Rugby in the early 1830s, was one of these.[29] Brother-in-law to Stanley and appointed Head Master of Harrow in 1845, he remodelled the school on Arnoldian lines and in fourteen years increased its numbers from 69 to 469.[30] Although he was the only one of Arnold's pupils to become headmaster of a Clarendon school, several others passed on the Arnoldian influence when they were appointed headmasters of other public schools:[31] *Henry Highton*, who entered Rugby in January 1829 and later, after eighteen years on the Rugby staff, became principal of Cheltenham College (1859–62); another of Arnold's earliest pupils, *A. H. Wratislaw*, who joined the school in August 1829, headmaster of Felsted School (1852–6) and then King Edward VI Grammar School, Bury St Edmund's (1856–79); *Thomas Burbidge*, Master of Leamington College (1851–7); *J. P. Gell*, appointed principal of the first Secondary College in Tasmania on Arnold's recommendation;[32] *J. D. Collis*, Master of Bromsgrove School (1843–67) and later founder and Warden of Stratford-on-Avon School; *R. G. Bryan*, Principal of Monkton Combe College, Bath (1875–1900), who greatly expanded its numbers; *D. W. Turner*, headmaster of the Liverpool Institution School (1846–74); *G. G. Bradley*, friend of the Arnold family who taught at Rugby for twelve years and was housemaster of one of the largest Houses before becoming Master of Marlborough (1858–70); *Henry Walford*, Head Master of Lancing (1859–61), who encouraged the Lancing boys to think that he was the original Slogger Williams of *Tom Brown's Schooldays*; *J. L. Brereton*, who founded West Buckland School in 1858, designed for middle-class parents living in the country who could not afford the fees of schools like Rugby;[33] and *E. H. Bradby*, Master of Haileybury (1868–83) after a period on Vaughan's staff at Harrow, described by Montagu Butler as a 'Rugbeian of the Rugbeians'.

Even more effective in the spread of this influence elsewhere were members of Arnold's staff or those who taught at Rugby later. It is indeed a further tribute to him that his ten assistants at the time of his death all held him in such high regard. *Cotton's* achievement at Marlborough has already been touched on in Chapter 6; but *James Prince Lee*, Arnold's right-hand man on the Rugby staff from 1830 to 1838, then headmaster of King Edward's, Birmingham till 1848, not only took Arnold's spirit and ideals there but passed on that influence to his pupil, *E. W. Benson,* who later taught at Rugby under Dr Goulburn, and as Master of Wellington (1859–68) established its reputation.[34] Two other assistant masters, *Henry Hill*, teaching at Rugby from 1836 to 1842, who became Headmaster of Warwick School in the year of Arnold's death (1842–78),[35] and *John Penrose* (1839–46), Master of an Exmouth school (1846–72), also spread the Arnoldian influence. *John Percival*, briefly on the Rugby staff under Dr Temple and effectively the first Head Master of Clifton (1862–78), put this college firmly on the educational map, and was in turn succeeded by *J. M. Wilson* (1879–90), who had before his appointment served for twenty years on the Rugby staff. Percival returned to Rugby as Head Master in 1887, succeeding an old Rugbeian of Tait's time, *T. W. Jex-Blake*, who had himself earlier been an assistant master at Rugby (1858–68) and later a notable headmaster of Cheltenham (1868–74). Haileybury had as headmasters (in addition to Bradby mentioned above) *A. G. Butler*, a boy at Rugby under Arnold's successor Tait and assistant master under Temple from 1862 to 1867, and *James Robertson* (1884–90), also a Rugby master. *A. W. Potts*, also on Temple's staff (1862–70), was the founding headmaster of Fettes, dying in office in November 1889. Two other Rugby masters, *J. S. Phillpotts* and *F. E. Kitchener*, both appointed by Dr Temple in 1862, served for twelve years before becoming headmasters of Bedford School and Newcastle High School respectively. Finally, *R. W. Taylor*, on the Rugby staff from 1869 to 1877 under Hayman and Jex-Blake, was Headmaster of Kelly College from 1877 to 1886.

The ripples went wider still: Rossall's first headmaster, *John Woolley* (1844–9), an Oxford friend of Stanley, took Arnold as his model; *S. A. Pears*, who as headmaster of Repton from 1854–1874 increased its numbers from 50 to 250, had been much influenced as a Harrow housemaster by Vaughan, as also was *F. W. Farrar*, Master of Marlborough (1871–6), popular novelist and later Dean of Canterbury. *F. W. Walker*, Headmaster first in Manchester, then High Master of St Paul's (1877–1905), a day boy at Rugby under Tait, also promoted Arnoldian ideals. *H. G. Hart*, probably Sedbergh's most distinguished headmaster (1880–1900), who had been educated at Rugby under Tait, and was later an assistant master at Haileybury under the two Old Rugbeians A. G. Butler and E. H. Bradby, introduced Rugby football and followed Arnold's example in transferring school services from the local church to a newly built chapel. Two other headmasters, with no direct connection with Arnold, *B. H. Kennedy* (Shrewsbury, (1836–66) and *George Moberly* (Winchester, 1836–66), who have already been mentioned, also paid tribute to Arnold's inspiration.

Even on some Nonconformist schools, too, Arnold's influence can be traced. Bootham, the Quaker School in York, had at its head from 1829 to 1865 John Ford, on whom 'the spirit of Rugby's great master wrought ... with great power'.[36] Moreover, one of Nonconformist Mill Hill's early headmasters, Thomas Priestley (1835–53), corresponded with Arnold to learn how to run his school and introduced some of his ideas in a modified form.[37] Thus at over twenty public schools during the second half of the nineteenth century, through headmasters who had been masters or pupils at Rugby or in some way connected with them, Arnold's spirit was widely felt.

The pupil, however, who more than any other except Stanley made Dr Arnold famous was Thomas Hughes, author of the hugely popular *Tom Brown's Schooldays*, first published in 1857.[38] Nevertheless, what Lionel Trilling aptly called the Rugby *Iliad*[39] (for it is indeed the archetypal school story of the heroic age) conveys the picture of a very different school from Stanley's, and it is no surprise that the latter said of it: 'It is an absolute revelation to me; opens a world of which, though so near me, I was utterly ignorant.'[40] In later life he accepted that it was 'a faithful picture of the rougher side of school life as it presented itself in the earlier days of our great Head Master'. Though Hughes had eight years at Rugby and his last half-year was February–June 1841, with Stanley and Vaughan in the Sixth Form when he was a new boy and Clough his fag-master, though Bradley, and Matthew and Thomas Arnold, were contemporaries and he admired their father himself, he seems largely unaware of the Doctor's ideals for his Sixth Form. The order of Tom Brown's aims indeed, as expressed to Arthur whom he is supposed to be looking after, is precisely the opposite of his headmaster's: sporting, intellectual, moral.[41] It is, however, a valuable corrective to Stanley's portrait, inasmuch as it shows a more human Arnold and the ordinary boys' reaction to him.[42] Less high-minded, more down to earth, full of vigour and life, it describes most of those evils which Arnold associated with boarding-schools and worked hard to eradicate. Although its picture of Rugby in Arnold's time is accurate so far as it goes and was recognized as such by several of Hughes's contemporaries, it is altogether inadequate.[43] For it gives no hint of Arnold's intellectual powers or of his concern for the mind and his respect for learning. It emphasizes his more obvious qualities such as exuberance and kindness but lays insufficient stress on his subtlety and fanaticism. It emphasizes, too, the importance to boys of courage and self-reliance subordinated to Christian principles, but at a somewhat superficial level. The muscular Christianity that Hughes admired and portrayed was his, not Arnold's, ideal. Yet Hughes's picture is that which has established itself generally as characteristic of the nineteenth-century public school.[44] With no intention of being disloyal to his revered headmaster, Hughes's account in fact shows how far the school falls short of the Arnoldian ideal described by Stanley.[45] It may have been or seemed a temple of industrious peace to a few rare spirits like Stanley, but for most ordinary boys Hughes, who had been a typical schoolboy, described the school they knew—'a turbulent, tough, bullying life'. Many years later, however, in February 1891, as we saw in Chapter 6, Hughes's summary of what he had come to consider the average boy took away from Rugby in 1841 was rather different.[46] In the light of Stanley's *Life* and all that had been written about Arnold in the fifty years since his death, he had modified his first view or at least was now ready to place greater emphasis than he had in *Tom Brown's Schooldays* on Arnold's crusade to Christianize the boys. But what that testimony brings out prominently is the full extent of the influence of Arnold that Hughes and his contemporaries recognized towards the end of their lives as having affected them when they were young.[47]

In their own way, too, the later careers of Arnold's own children confirm this. All the boys, apart from Walter, the youngest, had the dubious advantage of being educated at the school while their father was its headmaster. With so powerful a personality at its head, it is perhaps remarkable that not only were their lives there so normal but also that later, except for Walter, who had a financial career, they showed so much interest in education. Matthew, through his writings much more widely known and generally influential than his father, made his living as an inspector of schools for thirty-five years and in his essays promoted ideals identical to his father's; Thomas helped organize schools in Tasmania, Edward was an inspector of schools in the West Country, and William was the first Director of Public Instruction in Punjab. Jane, too, his eldest child and particular confidante, passed on indirectly her father's influence, for she married W. E. Forster, a near neighbour in the Lakes who much admired her father and was author in 1870 of the first great Education Act.[48] That Arnold's views on the importance of bringing education to the working classes were given practical effect, to some extent at least, by his son-in-law can hardly be disputed.[49]

Part of the letter from the Dean of Salisbury to Sir Joshua Fitch quoted earlier provides an apt conclusion: 'When I first entered the University of Oxford I found there was a disposition on the part of many to undervalue the leading characteristics of Rugby men. It may have been true that Arnold's power was sometimes felt too keenly, and that grave problems difficult of solution were at times approached by young men who had hardly mastered their importance. But when I remember the earnest spirit and love of truth manifested . . . I seem to realize something of the Arnoldian afflatus.'[50]

10

CONCLUSION

Strictly interpreted, Dr Hawkins's prophecy that Arnold would change the face of education all through the public schools of England was not fulfilled. As A. C. Percival has argued, it was the sort of remark that those who have written many testimonials recognize as typical of the genre.[1] It sounds good but means little. What did Hawkins mean by the public schools? In 1828 there were only seven, as we have seen; most of these never admitted Arnold's influence. Indeed Eton, for example, prided itself on escaping it. The public schools that were most affected were founded after his death.

'The face of education' had even less meaning. Arnold, as the last chapter made clear, introduced no major curricular or administrative reforms. Even if education is interpreted more widely, and Hawkins's phrase rewritten to mean that Arnold changed the educational face of the public schools, it is still wide of the mark. For he altered little of the outward aspects of their life. Apart from the replacement of dames by housemasters and the special trust he put in his prefects, no specific improvements can be credited to him. As J. Chandos has suggested, of the four main nineteenth-century reforms in public schools—the broadening of the curriculum including the promotion of the study of science, the development of compulsory, organized games, the uniformity of dress, and the stricter social discipline and close moral surveillance—Arnold was opposed to part of the first and indifferent to the second and third.[2]

In the fourth, however, lies the clue to his reputation. While he is often criticised[3] for the worst aspects of prefectorial government and athleticism as they developed in the public schools in the later part of the nineteenth century, and the Arnold myth continues to be based on these misconceptions, his main achievement was to re-establish confidence in the public schools, to put heart into a moribund system. This, as we saw in the last chapter, he effected by his single-minded, fierce determination to turn out Christian gentlemen. Though he himself at times doubted the value of a boarding education, chiefly because of the removal of parental influence on adolescent boys, he tried to supply this deficiency himself by his patriarchal attitude to his pupils. Despite his constant concern with the wider issues of his time, social, political, and theological, he made it his chief task to Christianize the school. For him education was primarily the religious and moral training of character.[4]

Through this activity and all that flowed from it his achievement was threefold: first, he confirmed Rugby's reputation as one of England's leading public schools; secondly, by thus strengthening the morale of the other public schools and giving an impetus to the foundation of new ones, he established the idea of the individual boarding-school;[5] thirdly, he secured the position of headmasters of these schools, establishing their independence and authority.

First, Rugby's reputation. T. W. Bamford has plausibly argued that, in addition to the striking effects of Stanley's biography and Hughes's school story on public opinion, two other circumstances helped to make Arnold's reputation wider than that of other notable nineteenth-century headmaster: the spread of Rugby football and the archiepiscopal careers of two of his successors.

Though William Webb Ellis, a Foundationer under Dr Wooll, is credited with inventing the game in 1823, and royal interest in it was shown as early as 1839, what gave Rugby football a national reputation was the enthusiastic description in *Tom Brown's Schooldays* by Hughes, to whom the game was the heart of public school life, followed later by its introduction into those public schools whose headmasters had been on Arnold's staff. These spread the game and the name of the school together.

The school's position was still further reinforced by the elevation to the Archbishopric of Canterbury of two headmasters who succeeded Arnold: A. C. Tait, a Balliol tutor, Head Master of Rugby 1842–50, and Frederick Temple, Head Master 1858–69.[6] Though Arnold himself cannot of course be directly credited with their promotion, would men of such calibre have applied for the post of headmaster if they had not been influenced by the school's fame and that of the headmaster who had so recently re-established it?

Though an examination of Arnold's contribution to the theological and political controversies of his day has deliberately been omitted in this short study, his fierce and public debates, in particular with Newman and his followers, had brought his name to a much wider audience than would have been likely if he had restricted his energies to headmastering and writing books on ancient history. Thus after his death the developments in the ethos and customs of public schools tended to be associated with his name, regardless of whether they were due to his initiative or not.

His second major achievement is more questionable, for by strengthening the morale of public schools and making individual boarding-schools such a power on the educational scene that within twenty years of his death nine had been founded,[7] he could be blamed for preventing the development of a national system of day schools.[8] This had to wait until 1902 and has never been as effective as it would have been if public schools had not coexisted. Sir Michael Sadler, in his introduction to Arnold Whitridge's excellent biography of Arnold, contrasts the German and English responses during the critical years 1810–40 to the challenge of would-be educational reformers.[9] In England, Parliament

> failed to recast her system of public schools upon broad national lines under the supervision of the State, and left the way open for headmasters of genius to breathe new life and purpose into individual boarding schools. ... Samuel Butler and Arnold did for England what Wilhelm von Humboldt did for Prussia. Each in his own country impressed national opinion with a new ideal of public school training. Humboldt had all the power of government at his command, and produced a system: Arnold and Butler, with no aid from the state, made single schools a power in English education. Humboldt could so lay his plans as to embrace the whole of the middle and upper classes. Arnold and Butler had to be content to limit their reforms to the narrow sphere of a single school. Both Humboldt and Arnold thought primarily of character as the outcome of a high-spirited education. But Humboldt, because his plans of reform were designed for day schools, laid the chief stress on the formation of mind and character through an exciting course of intellectual training, and paid no regard to the influence of corporate life; while Arnold, because he had set himself to the reform of boarding schools, kept first in his mind the influence of boys on boys in a small and nearly self-contained society, and ... laid less emphasis on the intellectual than on the moral factors in the problem.
>
> [By 1837 Prussia had a] system of public schools which equipped the boys of the whole of the middle and upper classes with the knowledge, method, thoroughness, and power of co-operation needed for administration, commerce, and industry in the modern State: Arnold and his followers developed the boarding school at the cost of the day school, instilled into the upper middle classes a new sense of responsibility for

public welfare and trained . . . the generation which set the standards of duty in the new civil service and in local government. Prussia staked everything on a new model of public school; England did not cut herself loose from the older traditions of school life. The Prussian reform was vigorous, innovating, comprehensive; the English, slow, conservative and piecemeal.[10]

Arnold, aiming at the reconciliation, not the realignment, of classes, was in no way opposed to a national system of secondary day schools for the education of the middle classes; indeed he considered it 'a question of the greatest national importance' that they should have an education with advantages comparable to those enjoyed by the richer classes at public schools.[11] But he recognized that to establish such a system required government action, and temperamentally he disliked the centralization of state control.[12] Had he been concerned with educational reform in the wider sense, he would surely have supported the establishment of state secondary schools.

His third major achievement stemmed from his determination to be independent. His insistence on a headmaster's freedom to expel or remove those he wished, to speak his mind on public controversies whether educational or not, to be in full command of his school, strengthened the authority and independence of nineteenth-century headmasters and has continued to do so since. That headmasters of public schools today are so much more independent than most of their colleagues in maintained schools must be credited to Arnold more than most other headmasters of his century.

It is an independence that headmasters value highly. To have the full confidence of one's governors but at the same time to be aware that its continuance depends on how well one runs their school concentrates the mind wonderfully and elicits a headmaster's best. The smaller the trust given by a governing body to their headmaster, the less effective he is likely to be. A school needs, for successful governance, an undivided command. Committees have a useful advisory or consultative role, especially in matters of broad policy or in evolving detailed administrative changes, but a headmaster must be allowed to have his freedom of executive action as far as possible untrammelled.

Arnold was all for independence but not opposed to co-operation with other colleagues. In December 1834 he wrote to J. T. Coleridge of his hope of persuading several headmasters, including those of Eton and Harrow, to compose Greek and Latin grammars for general use in English schools. A year later, in January 1835, he was suggesting to Dr Longley of Harrow the need for more joint action. 'I do not like the centralizing plan of compulsory uniformity under the government; but I do not see why we should all be acting without the least reference to one another. Something of this kind is wanted, particularly I think with regard to expulsion.'[13] Nothing came of this initiative and it was left to Thring, headmaster of Uppingham, thirty-four years later to launch the Headmasters' Conference in 1869, which ever since has provided that link between headmasters which Arnold was looking for. This, too, has notably helped to strengthen headmasters' authority *vis-à-vis* their governors and their schools.

Any detailed analysis, however, of Arnold's achievement or attempt to explain his subsequent reputation by reference to particular reforms or ideas fails to account adequately for it. He achieved what he did because fundamental to his powerful intellect, determined personality, and Utopian idealism was his deep Christian faith. This was at the heart of his day-to-day dealings with boys. As Arnold Whitridge put it, 'he translated the most trivial events in everyday life as well as the most momentous political problems into adventures of righteousness'.[14] He had the gift of inspiring enthusiasm among the young.[15] The urgency, vitality, vigour, compassion so characteristic of him stemmed directly from his devotion to the person of Christ.

The young always respond to real conviction, though it must be conviction of the head as well as of the heart, and Arnold had both. Confused he may have been in some of his views, as Trilling suggests,[16] and paradoxical in some of his attitudes (as we saw in Chapter 1), but fundamentally he knew where he stood and why he stood there, and would explain this to his pupils. For the most part they either accepted his values or at the very least respected him for his stand. In today's world, few acknowledge any role for the priest, or in a school for the chaplain, except as filling in where the doctor, the psychiatrist, the social worker, and all the other ancillary officers of our welfare state leave off. It is less easy for us, in a secular, materialist, humanist world which emphasizes the importance of the specialist in so many respects, in education, in commerce and industry, in leisure, to see how a priest's value to society depends on his not allowing himself to become a specialist.

For only thus can he help to restore man's consciousness of the wholeness of his nature and so bridge the divisions and heal the tensions which have made for individual and collective schizophrenia. Every generation, as Ranke has claimed, is no doubt equidistant from eternity, but in the first half of the nineteenth century eternity was a far more pressing consideration than it seems today. Arnold's emphasis on his role as chaplain still has its influence. Governors of modern public schools, in requiring their headmasters to be communicant members of the Church of England or of Churches in communion therewith, tacitly acknowledge this. Although most parents regard religious worship and teaching as much less important than success in academic examinations, than good discipline, up-to-date buildings and equipment, and pleasant living conditions, it is characteristic of the best public schools that they still give a much higher priority to the religious dimension than does most of their clientele. Is it altogether fanciful and unworldly to believe that the continuing strength of these schools owes much more to this than is commonly supposed? Certainly that would have been Arnold's belief. God had called him to make Rugby a Christian school. This was fundamental in all that he did and tried to do.

Dr Percival, one of Arnold's successors as Head Master of Rugby (1887–95), who had earlier been an assistant master at the school, summed up his achievement by calling him 'a great prophet among schoolmasters rather than an instructor or educator . . . the secret of his power consisting not so much in the novelty of his ideas or methods, as in his commanding and magnetic personality'.[17] He was indeed no pedagogical theorist nor educational innovator, and the educational legacy with which he is often credited is for the most part not his. Other headmasters beside him believed in government through senior boys and in fagging, though none with the same moral earnestness. Although he valued physical exercise, he never advocated organized compulsory games. He is well described by Mr Chandos as 'a conspicuous public figure who dramatized *Life* as the Christian's battle against *Sin*'.[18] As such and in his desire to abbreviate the period of adolescence and hurry the young on to manhood, he is very different from headmasters today. A modern headmaster of a boys' public school, with an age range of 13–18 similar to Arnold's Rugby, is a specialist in adolescence. He knows how much most of his pupils long to experiment, to discover their identity by trial and error, to test the beliefs of adults. His charges need room to grow, but they also need an encompassing structure, a framework, firm but flexible, interpreted to them with imagination and sensitivity. Within this structure they can try out their ideas without too much damage to themselves or others. Yet at the same time most boys are essentially conservative in outlook and resist too much change or variety of activity. A headmaster has to encourage them to look beyond the immediate, to have a vision of what the future might hold for them and for their community. He hopes to develop their potential to the full to enable them not only to fit into adult society as it is but also to help change it for the better. It is his business to make the weak strong, and the strong gentle, so that when they come to implement their vision, or such aspects of it as are practicable, they do this effectively and sensitively. It is perhaps because of this lack of natural sympathy with adolescent boys that one may at first hesitate to call Arnold a great *headmaster*. But he was undoubtedly a major figure on the educational scene in the early nineteenth century, whose posthumous fame was largely the creation of a few of his ablest ex-pupils. Treated as adults at the age of 17 or 18 and entrusted with carrying out his policies, they responded to his trust with devoted enthusiasm. They saw combined in him, to an unusual degree, intellectual energy and curiosity, moral strength and idealism and a hatred of evil, severity and vehemence, a deep faith and piety, and a single-minded devotion to what he thought were their best interests.[19] These were the ingredients of that personality which, expressed in his sermons, letters, and other writings on Church and State, so impressed them that they were determined to secure his reputation as a great headmaster. Their judgement has surely been justified since, for despite reservations that can reasonably be made about his contributions to educational theory or practice, it was after all from within the setting of Rugby School and with the authority of his position there that he so continuously set forth his views and made his name.

There were of course other headmasters who also made names for themselves in the nineteenth century. The three most famous are Samuel Butler of Shrewsbury (1798–1836), brilliant classical scholar and teacher, John Keate of Eton (1809–34), notorious for flogging large numbers of his pupils, sometimes for no good reason, yet popular with the boys, and Edward Thring of Uppingham

(1853–87), educational reformer and founder of the Headmasters' Conference. Each in his own way fully deserves his reputation, but none of these three became, as did Arnold, 'a totem of the Victorian public school system',[20] nor are they, or any headmaster since then, as well or as widely known as Dr Arnold of Rugby. That is tribute enough.

APPENDIX A

DR ARNOLD'S CURRICULUM

	Classical Division.			Mathematical Division.	French Division.
	Language Time.	Scriptural Instruction, &c.	History Time.		
First Form	Latin Grammar, and Latin Delectus.	Church Catechism and Abridgment of New Testament History.	Markham's England, Vol. I.	Tables, Addition, Subtraction, Multiplication, and Division, simple and compound, Reduction.	Hamel's Exercises up to the auxiliary verbs.
Second Form	Latin Grammar and Latin Delectus. Eutropius.	St. Luke. Genesis.	Markham's England, Vol. II	The work done in the first form repeated; Rule of Three, Practice.	Hamel's Exercise, Auxiliary Verbs, regular Conjugations, and some of the irregular. Gaultier's Geography.

Third Form	Greek Grammar (Matthiæ Abridgment.) Valpy's Greek Exercises. Valpy's Greek Delectus. Florilegium. Translations into Latin.	Exodus, Numbers, Judges, I and II Samuel, St. Matthew.	Eutropius. Physical Geography, U.K.S.	Rule of Three. Practice. Vulgar Fractions. Interest.	Hamel's Exercises first Part continued, Irregular Verbs. Elizabeth, ou Les Exilés en Sibére.
Lower Remove	Greek Grammar, and Valpy's Exercises. Rules of the Greek Iambics. Easy Parts of the Iambics of the Greek Tragedians. Virgil's Eclogues. Cicero de Senectute.	St. Matthew in Greek Testament. Acts in the English Bible.	Parts of Justin. Parts of Xenophon's Anabasis. Markham's France to Philip of Valois.	Vulgar Fractions. Interest. Decimal Fractions. Square Root.	Hamel continued and repeated. Jussieu's Jardin des Plantes.

	Classical Division.			Mathematical Division.	French Division.
Fourth Form	Æschylus, Prometh. Virgil, Æn. II and III. Cicero de Amicitiâ.	Acts in the Greek Testament. St. John in the English Bible. Old Testament History.	Part of Xenophon's Hellenics. Florus, from III. 21. to IV. 11. History of Greece, U.K.S. Markham's France, from Philip of Valois. Detailed Geography of Italy and Germany.	Decimals, Involution and Evolution, Addition, Subtraction, Multiplication, and Division of Algebra. Binomial Theorem. Euclid, Book I, Propos. I to XV.	Hamel's 2nd Part, chiefly Syntax of the Pronouns. La Fontaine's Fables.
Upper Remove	Sophocles' Philoct. Æschyl. Eumenid. Homer's Iliad, I. II. Virgil Æn, IV, V. Parts of Horace, Odes I., II., III. Parts of Cicero's Epistles.	St. John in Greek Testament. Deuteronomy and Ep. of St. Peter. Selections from the Psalms.	Parts of Arrian. Parts of Paterculus, Book II. Sir J. Mackintosh's England.	Equation of Payments, Discount, Simple Equations. Euclid, Book I from XV to end.	Translations from English into French. La Fontaine's Fables.

Lower Fifth	Æschyl. Sept. contra Thebas. Sophocl. Œd. Tyr. Homer's Iliad, III. IV. Virgil's Æn., VI. VII. Extracts from Cicero's Epistles. Parts of Horace.	St. John. Epistles to Timothy and Titus. Bible History from 1 Kings to Nehemiah inclusive.	Parts of Arrian. Herodotus III., 1, 38, 61, 67, 88, 116. Livy, Parts of, II & III. Hallam's Middle Ages, France, Spain, Greeks, and Saracens. Physical and Political Geography of all Europe.	Exchange, Alligation, Simple Equations, with two unknown Quantities and Problems. Euclid, Book III.	Syntax and Idioms. A Play of Molière, to construe, and then turn again from English into French.
Fifth Form	Æschyl. Agamemn. Homer's Iliad, V. VI. Odyssey, IX. Demosthenes' Leptines in Aphobum. I. Virgil's Æn., VIII. Parts of Horace. Cicero in Verrem.	Epistles to the Corinthians. Paley's Horæ Paulinæ.	Parts of Herodotus and Thucydides. Parts of Livy. Hallam's Middle Ages. State of Society.	Quadratic Equations. Trigonometry. Euclid, to the end of Book VI.	Penées de Pascal. Translations from English into French.

APPENDIX A *(Continued)*

	Classical Division.			Mathematical Division.	French Division.
Sixth Form	Various Parts of Virgil and Homer. Some one or more of the Greek Tragedies. One or more of the private Orations of Demosthenes. Cicero against Verres. Parts of Aristotle's Ethics.	One of the Prophets in the Septuagint Version. Different Parts of the New Testament.	Parts of Thucydides, and Arrian. Parts of Tacitus. Parts of Russell's Modern Europe.	Euclid, III–VI. Simple and Quadratic Equations, Plane Trigonometry, Conic Sections.	Parts of Guizot's Histoire de la Révolut. de l'Angleterre, and Mignet's Histoire de la Révolut. Franç.

APPENDIX B

SUMMARY OF MAIN WORKS BY DR ARNOLD IN ORDER OF PUBLICATION

1829–34	*Sermons*, 3 volumes (1829, 1832, 1834). (Reprinted in 1878 in Mrs Foster's edition.)
1829	*The Christian Duty of Conceding the Claims of the Roman Catholics*. (Reprinted in 1845 in *Miscellaneous Works*.)
1830	Thucydides' *History of the Peloponnesian War*, first volume of edition.
1832	Thirteen letters on the social condition of the operative classes. (Reprinted in *Miscellaneous Works*.)
1832	Second volume of edition of Thucydides.
1833	*Principles of Church Reform*. (Reprinted in *Miscellaneous Works*.)
1835	Third volume of edition of Thucydides.
1836	'The Oxford Malignants'.
1838–42	*History of Rome*, 3 volumes (1838, 1840, 1842).
1841	An inaugural lecture on the study of modern history. Fourth volume of *Sermons*.
1842	*Introductory Lectures on Modern History*. Fifth volume of *Sermons*.
1845	*Miscellaneous Works* collected and republished:

- *The Christian Duty of Conceding the Claims of the Roman Catholics* (1829).
- On the Social Progress of States (1830).
- Extracts from *The Englishman's Register* (1831).
- Letters to *Sheffield Courant* (1831, 1832):
    1. The Social Condition of the Operative Classes (13 letters).
    2. The Education of the Middle Classes (2 letters).
    3. Reform and its Future Consequences (1 letter).
    4. The Election (2 letters).
- Preface to *Poetry of Common Life* (1831).
- *Principles of Church Reform*, with postscript (1831).
- Rugby School—Use of the Classics (*Quart. Journ. Ed.* vii, No. XIV (1834), 234–49).

'On the Discipline of Public Schools' (*Quart. Journ. Ed.* ix, No. XVIII (1835), 280–92).

Preface to the third volume of the edition of Thucydides (1835).

Lecture, 'On the Divisions and Mutual Relations of Knowledge' (1838).

'Order of Deacons' (1841).

Letters to *Hertford Reformer* (1837–41).

1847 Thucydides' *History of the Peloponnesian War*, with notes (with indices by Revd. R. P. G. Tiddeman, 1868).

1848 *History of the Roman Republic*, Introductory Dissertation, Chs. XIII–XIX, XXI.

History of the Roman Empire, Ch. II, Part I; Ch. IV, Part II; Ch. V, Part I; Ch. VI, Part II.

1878 *Sermons* in six volumes revised by his daughter, Mrs W. E. Foster:

I (1820–8) Laleham Sermons.
II (1828–31) Rugby Sermons.
III (1831–4) Rugby Sermons.
IV (1835–40) Rugby Sermons.
V (1841–2) Rugby Sermons.
VI (1832–40) Sermons chiefly on the interpretation of Scripture.

APPENDIX C

CHRONOLOGICAL OUTLINE OF DR ARNOLD'S LIFE

1795	Born at Cowes, Isle of Wight (seventh child), 13 June.
1800–3	Educated by Miss Delafield.
1801	Father dies.
1803	To Lord Weymouth's Grammar School, Warminster, September.
1807	To Winchester College.
1811	Elected Scholar of Corpus Christi College, Oxford. Joined College in Lent Term.
1812	His family moved from Isle of Wight to Kensington, March.
1814	Literae Humaniores (First Class).
1815	Elected Fellow of Oriel College, Oxford, 31 March. To Paris. Read English Prize Essay in Sheldonian Theatre at Oxford, 7 June.
1816	To France again. (In August his family moved to Hampton.)
1817	MA. Won Chancellor's Latin Essay Prize. To Germany.
1818	Visited the Lakes in the summer, met Wordsworth. Ordained Deacon, 20 December.
1819	Met Mary Penrose, daughter of Rector of Fledborough, Lincs., January. Leased house at Laleham on River Thames, and moved there from Hampton, August. Proposed to Mary Penrose, August. First pupils received in school run jointly with his brother-in-law, John Buckland, September.
1820	Married, 11 August.
1821	Began work on Lexicon of *Thucydides*. Jane (1) born (K), summer.
1822	Began work on History of Rome (Gracchi to Trajan), November. Matthew (2) born (Crab), 24 December.
1823	Thomas (3) born (Prawn), 30 November.

1824	Parted from Buckland, teaching older pupils. Daughter born but died in a few days. To the Lakes and Scotland.
1825	Mary (4) born (Bacco), 29 March. Visited Italy.
1826	Edward (5) born (Didu), 28 October. Toured Scotland.
1827	Failed to be elected to professorship at London University. Tour to Rome through France and Italy. Appointed Head Master of Rugby School, 10 December.
1828	William (6) born (Nidu), 7 April. Ordained priest. Toured Germany, June. Visited Rugby, 8–12 July. Left Laleham, 5 August. Settled at Rugby, 10 August. Doctor of Divinity, December.
1829	First volume of *Sermons* published, and *The Christian Duty of Conceding the Claims of the Roman Catholics*, February. Started writing reports to parents. Toured Switzerland and North Italy, July.
1830	First volume of *Thucydides* published, May. Toured France, Germany, Italy, Switzerland. Met Niebuhr. Susanna (7) born (Babbit), 30 August.
1831	Published *The Englishman's Register*: contributed thirteen letters to *Sheffield Courant* (1831–2). Built turret-stair to study. Became Chaplain to the school. Toured Scotland. Family holiday near Rydal, December.
1832	Second volume of *Sermons* published. Daughter born, April, but lived only seven days. Bought Fox How. School dispersed because of cholera. Trouble with *Northampton Herald* over episode of flogging of March.
1833	Frances (8) born (Bonze). *Principles of Church Reform* published, and second volume of *Thucydides*.
1834	Articles in *Quart. Journ. Ed.* and third volume of *Sermons* published. First holiday in Fox How, July.

1835	Third volume of *Thucydides* and *Quart. Journ. Ed.* article ('On the Discipline of Public Schools') published. Walter (9) born (Quid), 18 August. Fellow of London University.
1836	'The Oxford Malignants' published, April. Nearly dismissed by his Trustees, 4–4 vote. Sent two sons to Winchester.
1837	Letters to *Hertford Reformer* (to 1841). Visited France, August.
1838	First volume of *History of Rome* published. (First train drew into Rugby Station, 17 September.) Resigned London Fellowship, 7 November.
1839	Proposed to give up School House. Visited South of France. Visit to school by Queen Adelaide, 19 October. Two sermons on Prophecy and lecture *On the Divisions and Mutual Relations of Knowledge* published, November. Lord Langdale's judgement on Wratislaw case.
1840	Second volume of *History of Rome* published. Travelled to Rome and Naples.
1841	Fourth volume of *Sermons* published. Toured South of France. Elected Regius Professor of Modern History, Oxford. (Inaugural Lecture, 2 December.)
1842	Third volume of *History of Rome* and second edition of *Thucydides* published. Delivered eight *Introductory Lectures on Modern History*, in Oxford. Fifth volume of *Sermons* published. Died, aged 46, 12 June. Buried in Rugby School Chapel, 17 June.

APPENDIX D

SELECT BIBLIOGRAPHY

The Academy, Review of Sir Joshua Fitch's *Thomas and Matthew Arnold*, vol. 52 (1897).
Adamson, J. W., *English Education 1789–1902* (Cambridge 1930).
Alington, C. A., *A Schoolmaster's Apology* (London, 1914).
Annan, N. G., *Victorian Studies* (Edinburgh and London, 1927).
[Apperley, Charles James], *My Life and Times by Nimrod*, ed. E.D. Cuming (Edinburgh, 1927).
Arbuthnot, Sir Alexander J., *Memories of Rugby and India*, ed. Constance, Lady Arbuthnot (London, 1910).
Archer, R. L., *Secondary Education in the 19th Century* (Cambridge, 1921).
Arnold, Thomas, the younger, *Passages in a Wandering Life* (London, 1900).
Balston, Thomas, *Dr Balston at Eton* (London, 1952).
Bamford, T. W., *Thomas Arnold* (London, 1960).
—— *Thomas Arnold on Education* (Cambridge, 1970).
—— 'Discipline at Rugby under Arnold', *Educational Review*, Vol. 10, No. 1 (Nov. 1957).
—— 'Public School Town in the Nineteenth Century', *Brit. Journ. Educ. Studies*, No. 12 (1961).
—— 'Public Schools and Social Class 1801–1850', *Brit. Journ. Sociology*, No. 12, 1961.
—— *The Rise of the Public Schools* (London, 1967).
Barnett, Corelli, *The Audit of War* (London, 1986).
Bloxam, M. H., *Rugby, the School and Neighbourhood* (London, 1889).
Booth, J. B., *Bits of Character, A Life of Henry Hall Dixon* (London, 1936).
Bradby, H. C., *Rugby* (London, 1900).
Bradley, G. G., *Recollections of Arthur Penrhyn Stanley* (London, 1883).
—— *Six Great Schoolmasters* (London, 1904).
Brent, Richard, *Liberal Anglican Politics, 1830–1841* (Oxford, 1987).
Brett-James, N. G., *The History of Mill Hill School, 1807–1923* (Reigate, 1924).
Briggs, A., *Victorian People* (London, 1955).
Bulwer Lytton, Edward, *England and the English* (London, 1874).
Cahalin, B. J., *A Bibliography of Thomas Arnold* (High Wycombe, 1973).
Campbell, R. J., *Thomas Arnold* (London, 1927).

Chandos, J., *Boys Together* (London, 1984).
Christenson, M. A., 'Thomas Arnold's debt to German Theologians', *Modern Philology*, 55, No. 1 (Aug. 1957).
Clarendon Commission. *Report of Her Majesty's Commissioners appointed to inquire into the Revenues and Management of certain Colleges and Schools, and the Studies pursued and Instruction given therein*, vols. I–IV (1864).
Clough A. H., *The Correspondence*, ed. F. L. Mulhauser (Oxford, 1957).
Compton, B., *E. M. Goulburn, a memoir* (London, 1899).
Coulton, G. G., *A Victorian Schoolmaster: Henry Hart of Sedbergh* (London, 1923).
Dickinson, Charles, *Observations on Ecclesiastical Legislature and Church Reform* (Dublin, 1833).
Doyle, Sir Francis, *Reminiscences and Opinions, 1813–1885* (London, 1886).
Evers, C. R., *Rugby* (London, 1939).
Farrar, F. W., 'Thomas Arnold, DD', *Macmillan's Magazine*, vol. 37 (Nov.–Apr. 1878).
Findlay, J. J., *Arnold of Rugby: his School Life and Contributions to Education* (Cambridge, 1897).
Fitch, Sir Joshua, *Thomas and Matthew Arnold and their influence on English education* (London, 1897).
—— *Stanley's Life of Thomas Arnold*, Teachers' edn.: Introduction (London, 1901).
Forbes, D., *The Liberal Anglican Idea of History* (Cambridge, 1952).
Fox, G. T., *A Memoir of the Rev. H. W. Fox*, (London, 1850).
Fraser, G. M., ed., *The World of the Public School* (London, 1977).
Fremantle, W. R., *Memoir of the Rev. S. Thornton* (London, 1850).
Golding, William, 'Headmasters', *The Spectator*, No. 6894 (12 Aug. 1960).
Gooch, G. P., *History and Historians in the Nineteenth Century*, 2nd edn. (London, 1952).
[Gover, W.], 'Memories of Arnold and Rugby Sixty Years Ago in 1835, 1836, 1837', *The Parents' Review*, vols. 6 and 7 (1895–6).
Grant, W., Letters from Rugby 1791–6, MS in Temple Reading Room, Rugby School.
Grenfell, A., 'Diary', MS in Temple Reading Room, Rugby School.
Hamilton, Niall, 'A History of the Architecture and the ethos of the School Chapel', Ph.D. thesis, Bristol University, 1985.
Honey, J. R. de S., *Tom Brown's Universe* (London, 1977).
How, F. D., *Six Great Schoolmasters* (London, 1904).
Hughes, Thomas, *Tom Brown's Schooldays*, 6th edn. (London, 1858).
—— *Fifty Years Ago. A Layman's address to Rugby School, Quinquagesima Sunday, 1891* (London and New York, 1891).

Hughes, Thomas, *Great Public Schools* (London, 1894).
Jackson, M. J., and Rogan, J., *Thomas Arnold—Principles of Church Reform* (London, 1962).
Jowett, B., *Thucydides*, translated into English, vol. i. (Oxford, 1881).
Lake, Katharine, ed., *Memorials of William Charles Lake, Dean of Durham, 1869–1894* (London, 1901).
Lake, W. C., 'Rugby and Oxford', *Good Words*, Oct. 1895.
—— 'Stanley's Life of Arnold', Quarterly Review, vol. 74, No. 148 (Oct. 1844) and Vol. 102, No. 204, (1857).
Lindon, John, MS in Temple Reading Room, Rugby School.
MacCarthy, Desmond, *Portraits* (London 1931).
Mack, E. C., *Public Schools and British Opinion 1780–1860* (London, 1938).
—— and Armytage, W. H. G., *Thomas Hughes. The Life of the Author of Tom Brown's Schooldays* (London, 1952).
Macready, W. C., *Reminiscences and Selections from his Diaries and Letters*, ed. Sir. F. Pollock (London, 1875).
Maison, M. M., 'Tom Brown and Company', *English*, vol. 12 (autumn, 1958).
Maitland, E., 'The Life and Correspondence of Thomas Arnold, DD, late Head Master of Rugby School, and Regius Professor of Modern History in the University of Oxford' *The North British Review*, Vol. II, No. 4, (Feb. 1845).
Mangan, J. A., *Athleticism in the Victorian and Edwardian Public School: the emergence and consolidation of an educational ideology* (Cambridge, 1981).
Marten, C. H. K., *On the Teaching of History* (Oxford, 1938).
Martineau, J., *Essays, Reviews, and Addresses*, 3 vols. (London, 1890).
Melly, G., *School Experiences of a Fag at a Private and a Public School* (London, 1854).
Moyer, C. R., 'The idea of History in Thomas and Matthew Arnold', *Modern Philology*, 67, No. 2 (1969–70).
Mozley, J. B., *Essays historical and theological*, vol. ii (London, 1878).
Murry, John Middleton, *The Price of Leadership* (London, 1939).
Neander, A., *The Theology of Thomas Arnold, its importance and bearing on the present state of the Church* (Cambridge, 1846).
Newsome, D., *Godliness and Good Learning* (London, 1961).
—— *A History of Wellington College, 1859–1959* (London, 1959).
Nicholls, D., 'The Totalitarianism of Thomas Arnold', *Review of Politics*, Vol. 29 (Oct. 1967).
Ogilvie, V., *The English Public School* (London, 1957).
Oldham, J. B., *A history of Shrewsbury School, 1552–1952* (Oxford, 1952).

Oswell, W. E., *William Cotton Oswell, Hunter and Explorer* (London, 1900).

Parents' Review, The: See under Gover, W.

Pattison, M., *Memoirs* (London, 1885).

Payne, W. M., 'Thomas and Matthew Arnold', review of *Arnold of Rugby* by J. J. Findlay and of *Thomas and Matthew Arnold* by Sir Joshua Fitch, *The Dial*, No. 280, Vol. xxiv (16 Feb. 1898).

Pell, Albert, *The Reminiscences of Albert Pell, sometime MP for South Leicestershire*, ed. with introd. by T. MacKay (London, 1908).

Percival, A. C., *Very Superior Men* (London, 1973).

Pollard, F. E., ed., *Bootham School, York, 1823–1923* (London, 1926).

Powell, Revd H. T., *Strictures on Dr Arnold's Pamphlet, entitled 'The Christian Duty of granting the claims of the Roman Catholics'* (London, 1829).

—— *Liberalism Unveiled; or strictures on Dr Arnold's Sermons* (London, 1830).

Prothero, R. E., and Bradley, G. G., *The Life and Correspondence of Arthur Penrhyn Stanley, DD* (London, 1893).

Quigly, I., *The heirs of Tom Brown* (London, 1982).

Radclyffe, C. W., *Memorials of Rugby* (Rugby, 1843).

Record, The. 'Brief Observations on the Political and Religious Sentiments of the late Rev. Dr Arnold', (London, 1845).

Roach, John, *A history of secondary education in England, 1800–1870* (London, 1986).

Rouse, W. H. D., *A History of Rugby School* (London, 1898).

Rugbaean, The, No. 1, Mar. (Rugby, 1840).

Rugby Advertiser, The, Oct. 1924.

Rugby Magazine, The, vols. i and ii (London, 1835–7).

Rugby Miscellany, The, Mar. 1845 (London, 1846).

Rugby Register, The, from 1675 (Rugby, 1829).

Sanders, C. R., *Coleridge and the Broad Church Movement* (Durham, NC, 1942).

—— *Lytton Strachey, his mind and art* (New Haven, 1957).

Selfe R. E., *Dr Arnold of Rugby* (London, 1889).

Selfe, Lt.-Col. S., *Notes on the Characters and Incidents depicted by the master hand of Tom Hughes in 'Tom Brown's Schooldays'* (Rugby, 1909).

Sidgwick, F., ed., *Tom Brown's Schooldays* (London, 1913).

Simon, B., and Bradley, I., *The Victorian Public School* (Dublin, 1975).

Stanley, Revd A. P., *The Life and Correspondence of Thomas Arnold, DD*, 2nd edn. of Minerva reprint of 6th edn. published in 1846 (London, 1890).

—— *A Sermon, preached in the Chapel of Rugby School*, (14 Aug. 1842) (Rugby, 1842).

Stanley, Revd A. P., 'Address delivered in Rugby School Chapel on Friday 12 June, 1874', *Macmillan's Magazine*, vol. xxx (May–Oct. 1874).

Stebbing, W., ed., *Charles Henry Pearson, Fellow of Oriel and Education Minister in Victoria. Memorials by himself, his wife, and his friends* (London, 1900).

Stephen, J. F., 'Tom Brown's Schooldays' *Edinburgh Review*, vol. 107, No. 217 (Jan.–Apr. 1858).

Strachey, G. L., *Eminent Victorians* (London, 1918).

Stuart, Hon. A. G., *Examination of a Tract Entitled 'Brief Observations on the political and religious sentiments of the late Rev. Dr Arnold,&c.'* (London, 1845).

Temple, The Rt. Hon. Sir Richard, Bt., *The Story of My Life* (London, 1896).

Trevor, M., *The Arnolds: Thomas Arnold and His Family* (London, 1973).

Trilling, L., *Matthew Arnold* (London, 1939).

Trotter, L. J., *A Leader of Light Horse* (Edinburgh, 1901).

Turner, Frank M., *The Greek Heritage in Victorian Britain* (New Haven and London, 1981).

Vaughan, C. J., *A funeral sermon on Arthur Penrhyn Stanley preached in Westminster Abbey, July 24, 1881* (London, 1881).

—— *A letter to the Viscount Palmerston on the monitorial system of Harrow School*, and reply (London, 1854).

Walrond, T., entry on Arnold in *Dictionary of National Biography*, vol. 11 (London, 1885).

Ward, Sir A. W., entries in *Cambridge History of English Literature*, vol. 12 (Cambridge, 1915), ch. xiv.

Ward, W. P., *William George Ward and the Oxford Movement* (London, 1889).

Whitridge, A., *Dr Arnold of Rugby* (London, 1928).

Willey, B., *The English moralists* (London, 1964).

—— *Nineteenth Century Studies* (London, 1949).

—— *More Nineteenth Century Studies* (London, 1956).

—— *Christianity, Past and Present* (London, 1952).

Williamson, E. L., *The Liberalism of Thomas Arnold; a study of his religious and political writings* (Alabama, 1964).

Woodward, E. L., *The Age of Reform 1815–1870* (Oxford, 1938).

Woodward, F. J., *The Doctor's Disciples* (Oxford, 1954).

Worboise, E. J., *Life of Thomas Arnold, DD* (London, 1859).

Wordsworth, C., *Annals of My Early Life 1806–1846* (London, 1891).

Wymer, N. G., *Dr Arnold of Rugby* (London, 1953).

Yates, J., *Remarks on Dr Arnold's 'Principles of Church Reform'* (London, 1833).

Young, G. M., ed., *Early Victorian England, 1830–1865*, 2 vols. (London, 1934).

NOTES

(to pages 1–4)

CHAPTER 1

1. Norman Wymer, *Dr Arnold of Rugby*, 85.
2. M. Trevor, *The Arnolds: Thomas Arnold and His Family* (1973), 22; Arnold Whitridge, *Dr Arnold of Rugby*, 54. Cf. A. P. Stanley, *The Life and Correspondence of Thomas Arnold, DD*, 2nd edn. of Minerva reprint of 6th edn., (1890), 49, which is an under-estimate.
3. Stanley, *Life*, 30.
4. E. Maitland, *The North British Review*, Feb. 1945, 407; W. C. Lake, *Quarterly Review*, LXXIV Oct. 1844, 471; Whitridge, op. cit. 19–23. Oriel College at that period had Copleston as Provost and among its Fellows Whately, Davison, Hawkins, Hampden, and Keble; Newman and Pusey were elected soon after, in 1822 and 1823 respectively.
5. Stanley, *Life*, 18.
6. Ibid. 27.
7. Ibid. 18.
8. Ibid. 343.
9. Ibid. 379.
10. Ibid. 23; W. C. Lake, loc. cit. 470.
11. Stanley, *Life*, 55.
12. Ibid. 54.
13. Ibid. 22–3.
14. Ibid. 108; Fitzjames Stephen, *Edinburgh Review*, vol. cvii (Jan. and Apr. 1858), 183. 'The special peculiarity of his character would seem to have been an intense and somewhat impatient fervour. To him and his admirers we owe the substitution of the word "earnest" for its predecessor "serious".' David Newsome, *Godliness and Good Learning* (1961), 19.
15. Stanley, *Life*, 393.
16. Ibid. 242–3.
17. Ibid. 320.
18. Ibid. 31.
19. Edward C. Mack, *Public Schools and British Opinion 1780–1860*, 242. Lytton Strachey's *Eminent Victorians* (1918) is a skilful exercise in falsification. In particular his maliciously tendentious attack on Dr Arnold is too extreme a caricature to be regarded as a serious criticism of its subject. Strachey had suffered much at three minor public schools and could therefore find nothing to admire in one who had been headmaster of such an institution. He takes revenge for his past misery by portraying Arnold as an impostor and a clown. His essay is

now generally considered ludicrously exaggerated, distorted, and unfair.

20. This is perhaps better explained by Mrs Arnold's comment in her *Journal* that during the painting of the portrait by Phillips in 1839, Arnold had been so deeply engaged in discussion with Chevalier Bunsen and Crabbe Robinson about Niebuhr's *History of Rome* that the artist had called for silence.
21. Stanley, *Life*, 11–12, 340; James Martineau, *Essays, Reviews, and Addresses*, vol. 1 (1890), 50 ff; Trevor, op. cit. 35; E. L. Williamson, *The Liberalism of Thomas Arnold* (1964), 85; E. L. Woodward, *The Age of Reform 1815–1870* (1938), 467; F. J. Woodward, *The Doctor's Disciples* (1954), 1 ff.
22. Basil Willey, *Christianity, Past and Present* (1952), 3–4.
23. Stanley, *Life*, 175.
24. Williamson, op. cit. 76–7; F. J. Woodward, op. cit., facing p. 25.
25. Williamson, op. cit. 98 ff.
26. Ibid. 113, 121.
27. Thomas Arnold, *Miscellaneous Works* (1845), 259; Williamson, op. cit. 128.
28. Williamson, op. cit. 129.
29. Lionel Trilling, *Matthew Arnold* (1939), 58.
30. Whitridge, op cit. 171; Thomas Arnold, *Sermons* iii (1878), Appendix to sermon xi, 272.
31. Wilfred Ward, *William George Ward and the Oxford Movement* (1890), 49.
32. *Misc. Works*, 291.
33. W. C. Lake, loc. cit. 496. David Cecil, *Lord M* (London, 1954), 246. Arnold was considered for a bishopric by Lord Melbourne, but the Liberal Prime Minister preferred peace and quiet to new ideas, and the humourless, progressive Arnold represented much that he disliked.
34. *Misc. Works*, 332; Trilling, op. cit. 53.
35. Basil Willey, *Nineteenth Century Studies* (1949), 54.
36. Trilling, op. cit. 54.
37. Ibid. 49.
38. *Misc. Works*, 182.
39. Williamson, op. cit. 185.
40. Stanley, *Life*, 261.
41. Ibid., 261.
42. Trilling, op. cit. 53, 55.
43. *Misc Works*, 176–7; Williamson, op. cit. 186.
44. Trilling, op. cit, 50–1; T. Arnold, *Thucydides' History of the Peloponnesian War* (1840), vol. i, Appendix 1. 503, 521.
45. Williamson, op. cit. 190–2.
46. Duncan Forbes, *The Liberal Anglican Idea of History* (1952), 5.

47. Williamson, op. cit. 193–4.
48. Charles Dickinson, *Observations on Ecclesiastical Legislature and Church Reform* (1833), 30–2, on Arnold's confusion over Church and State.
49. Thomas Arnold, the younger, *Passages in a Wandering Life* (1900), 30; Richard Brent, *Liberal Anglican Politics, 1830–1841* (1987), 166–7.
50. Stanley, *Life*, 425.
51. Ibid. 129.
52. Wymer, op. cit. 145.
53. Stanley, *Life*, 34, 38.
54. Ibid. 358.
55. Ibid. 128.
56. Ibid. 409–10.
57. Ibid. 407.
58. Ibid. 129.
59. Thomas Arnold, the younger, *Passages*, 9.
60. Stanley, *Life*, 276.
61. Ibid. 197, 132.
62. Ibid. 132.
63. Ibid. 133.
64. Ibid. 181.
65. Ibid. 9.
66. Whitridge, op. cit. 46.
67. T. W. Bamford, *Thomas Arnold on Education* (1970), 4–5.
68. Mack, op. cit. 242.
69. Rowland E. Prothero and G. G. Bradley, *The Life and Correspondence of Arthur Penrhyn Stanley, DD*, vol. i (1893), 317–18; *Sermon on the Death of Dr Arnold*, preached in Rugby Chapel, Rugby, 1842.

CHAPTER 2

1. *Edinburgh Review* XVI (August 1810), 327, 330.
2. J. W. Adamson, *English Education 1789–1902* (1930), 66.
3. C. R. Evers, *Rugby* (1939), 26–7.
4. Macready, *Reminiscences*, ed. Sir Frederick Pollock, Bt. (1875), vol. I, 21.
5. J. J. Findlay, *Arnold of Rugby* (1897), 48.
6. Thomas Hughes, *Tom Brown's Schooldays* (1858), 102–3.
7. Ibid. 246–7. A 'fag' is a junior boy who does menial service for older boys.
8. Wymer, *Dr Arnold of Rugby*, 100.
9. Trustees' Order, 6 July 1830 confirming recommendation made by Dr Arnold in a letter of 29 June (in the Library of the University of Birmingham).

10. Stanley, *Life*, 233.
11. W. E. Oswell, *William Cotton Oswell, Hunter and Explorer* (1900), Vol. I, 51.
12. Stanley, *Life*, 396.
13. Ibid. 232. Wymer, op. cit. 176.
14. W. H. D. Rouse, *A History of Rugby School* (1898), 257–8; cf. Whitridge, *Dr Arnold of Rugby*, 129.
15. Hughes, op. cit. 180.
16. A ball game played with the hands by two or four players in a walled court.
17. Rouse, op. cit. 250.
18. Hughes, op. cit. 220–1.
19. Ibid. 162–3.
20. Ibid. 161, 188.
21. Ibid. 333–4.
22. Ibid. 137.

CHAPTER 3

1. Stanley, *Life*, 48.
2. Ibid. 365–6.
3. *Misc. Works*, 227–30; Bamford, *Thomas Arnold on Education*, 95–7.
4. Stanley, *Life*, 62.
5. Ibid. 135; cf. Fitch, *Thomas and Matthew Arnold and their influence on English Education*, 109.
6. Ibid. 50.
7. Ibid. 69; Newsome, *Godliness and Good Learning*, 34.
8. Hughes, *Tom Brown's Schooldays*, 80.
9. Whitridge, *Dr Arnold of Rugby*, xlvii; Findlay, *Arnold of Rugby*, 237.
10. The full text of Dr Moberly's letter is to be found on pp. 108–9.
11. Bamford, op. cit. 97–9, 100; Stanley, *Life*, 60.
12. Whitridge, op. cit. Appendix 1, 215 ff.
13. Stanley, *Life*, 280–1.
14. Ibid. 282.
15. Wymer, *Dr Arnold of Rugby*, 89; Stanley, *Life*, 53.
16. In his later years his salary from all sources amounted to at least £4,000 p.a., which would have made him a comparatively wealthy man. *Report of Her Majesty's Commissioners appointed to inquire into the Revenues and Management of certain Colleges and Schools and the Studies pursued and Instruction given therein* (1864), The Clarendon Commission, vol. i. 261; T. W. Bamford, *Thomas Arnold* (1960), 178.
17. Stanley, *Life*, 224.
18. *The Correspondence of Arthur Hugh Clough*, ed. Frederick L. Mulhauser, vol. i (1957), 43.

19. Trustees' Resolution, 23 March, 1836.
20. Clarendon Commission, *Report*, 232.
21. Letter to Lord Denbigh, unpublished, in Temple Reading Room, Rugby School.
22. Clarendon Commission, *Report*, 261–2.
23. Adamson, *English Education 1789–1902*, 249; Clarendon Commission, *Report*, 233.
24. Stanley, *Life*, 61 (*'vile damnum'*: 'a trifling loss'; ἐκ παρέργου means 'on the side'; πάρεργον, meaning 'secondary' or 'subordinate' business, was one of Arnold's favourite words).
25. Stanley, *Life*, 351.
26. Whitridge, op. cit. 100.
27. Algernon Grenfell, MA, 'Diary', Temple Reading Room, Rugby School.
28. Trustees' Order, 25 Oct. 1831.
29. Stanley, *Life*, 91, 350; Harrow Archives, letter from T. Arnold to C. Wordsworth, 31 May 1837.
30. In fact he devoted the salary to the establishment of a school library. Wymer, op. cit. 115; Stanley, *Life*, 91.
31. Fitch, op. cit. 97–9.
32. Hughes, op. cit. 141.
33. Wymer, op. cit. 187.
34. J. Omeris, letter, 9 Feb. 1843, in Temple Reading Room, Rugby School.
35. T. Arnold, letter to Mr Justice Coleridge, 16 Nov. 1838 (in Bodleian Library): 'But the wear and weariness to me arises from the Boarding House part of the business; and this I am strongly proposing to give up next summer. I think that as a general rule a Head Master ought to have no boarders. . . . I think that after more than ten years' work here I may rid myself of a part of the charge which is not naturally connected with my situation as Head Master, and which of all others is to me, especially as I grow older, the most irksome. I have a strong reluctance to going about among boys to see whether they are drinking, or sitting up too late, or otherwise in mischief; and the School House is more a pressure on my mind than all the school besides. Then again I am anxious to save my wife the uneasiness which she now is exposed to when the boys are not well. . . . I have long since, even from the time when I first came to Rugby, wished to get rid of the boarders, but certainly my feeling has been very much strengthened by the state of the School House during the present half year.'
36. *Sermons*, iv. iii. 20–1; J. Chandos, *Boys Together* (1984), 252–3; Sir Francis Doyle, *Reminiscences and Opinions, 1813–1835* (1886), 48.

37. Stanley, *Life*, 65; Bamford, *Thomas Arnold on Education*, 79–80.
38. Stanley, *Life*, 102.
39. Bamford, *Thomas Arnold on Education*, 104; cf. K. Lake, *Memorials of William Charles Lake, Dean of Durham, 1819–1894* (1901), 158–9.
40. Bamford, *Thomas Arnold on Education*, 144–150. For example, he freely gave advice on careers, pointing to the dangers of the Army and Navy, especially the temptation therein to prefer men's to God's praise. Personally attracted by the study of law and medicine, he nevertheless disapproved of their practice. Yet while abhorring the lawyer, he honoured the doctor.
41. Newsome, op. cit. 56; Bamford, *Thomas Arnold on Education*, 151, 163. London University he could not recommend because it avowed a principle to which he was totally opposed—that education need not be connected with Christianity.
42. Stanley, *Life*, 252.
43. Ibid. 238.
44. Ibid. 103.
45. Ibid. 49–50.
46. Hughes, op. cit. 137, 396.
47. Mack, *Public Schools and British Opinion 1780–1860*, 268.
48. Fitch, op. cit. 103–4; Aristole, *Politics*, viii. iii, 3–5.
49. J. A. Mangan, *Athleticism in the Victorian and Edwardian Public School* (1981), 17–18.
50. Sir Alexander J. Arbuthnot, *Memories of Rugby and India* (1910), 31–2.
51. Hughes, op. cit. 138.
52. Ibid. 136; Mack, op. cit. 332. 'In no other aspect of his book do we feel so strongly the cheapening of Arnold's conception of a Public School as in Hughes's insistance on the almost exclusive value of athlectics.'
53. Stanley, *Life*, 253; Rouse, *A History of Rugby School*, 247.
54. The first Rugby Debating Society was founded in 1833. Rouse, op. cit. 246.
55. Lt.-Col. Sydney Selfe, *Notes on the Characters and Incidents depicted by the master hand of Tom Hughes in 'Tom Brown's Schooldays'* (1909), 26; cf. P/A 20, letter of Mary Arnold to her sister, Brotherton Library B8210, Leeds.
56. Hughes, op. cit. 239.
57. Ibid. 242.
58. Prothero and Bradley, *Life and Correspondence of Stanley*, i. 45.
59. Albert Pell, *The Reminiscences of Albert Pell, sometime MP for South Leicestershire*, ed. T. MacKay (1908), 275. Trilling, *Matthew Arnold*, 44.

60. Trilling, *Matthew Arnold*, 44; F. J. Woodward, *The Doctor's Disciples* (1954), 183.
61. *Sermons*, ii. xxiii. 170–2. The public-school missions, established in London in the late nineteenth century, had a similar motivation.
62. Stanley, *Life*, 175.
63. Ibid. 98.
64. Ibid. 82; Wymer, op. cit. 186.
65. Stanley, *Life*, 269.
66. Ibid. 392.
67. Ibid. 459. The MS at Rugby School was inaccurately transcribed by Dr Stanley. '*Vixi*': 'I have lived my life'.
68. Clough, *Correspondence*, 118–19.
69. Algernon Grenfell, 'Diary', Temple Reading Room, Rugby School; Prothero and Bradley, op. cit. i. 311.

CHAPTER 4

1. Matthew Arnold, *Poems*, vol. ii. (1877), 246–8.
2. Hughes, *Tom Brown's Schooldays*, 157 ff.
3. Francis J. Woodward, *The Doctor's Disciples* (1954), 4.
4. Woodward, op. cit. 24.
5. Stanley, *Life*, 95.
6. *Sermons*, ii, xii. 80–83.
7. Stanley, *Life*, 28.
8. J. R. de S. Honey, *Tom Brown's Universe*, 25.
9. *Sermons*, ii. v. 33–4.
10. Stanley, *Life*, 154.
11. Chandos, *Boys Together*, 255–6; J. B. Booth, *Bits of Character, A Life of H. H. Dixon* (1936), 24.
12. Fitch, *Thomas and Matthew Arnold*, 87–8; Stanley, *Life*, 175.
13. Fitch, op. cit, 91.
14. Stanley, *Life*, 87.
15. Thomas Balston, *Dr Balston at Eton* (1952), 51.
16. Stanley, *Life*, 101.
17. Ibid. 456.
18. Clarendon Commission, *Report*, 259.
19. Fitch, op. cit. 92; G. T. Fox, *A Memoir of the Rev. H. W. Fox* (1850), 29, 31.
20. Lake, *Memorials* (1901), 9.
21. J. P. C. Roach, *A history of secondary education in England, 1800–1870* (1986), 246–7.
22. Woodward, op. cit. 77.
23. Stanley, *Life*, 91.
24. C. A. Alington, *A Schoolmaster's Apology* (1914), 114–5.

CHAPTER 5

1. Stanley, *Life*, 62–3, 79; Fitch, *Thomas and Matthew Arnold*, 96.
2. *Sermons*, ii. xxiii. 166–7.
3. Stanley, *Life*, 8.
4. Ibid. 82.
5. *Misc. Works*, 350; Fitch, op. cit. 37.
6. Thomas Arnold, Preface to the first edition of *Thucydides' History of the Peloponnesian War*, iii. xvi; Frank M. Turner, *The Greek Heritage in Victorian Britain* (1981), 26–7.
7. D. Forbes, *The Liberal Anglican Idea of History* (1952), 14.
8. G. M. Young, ed., *Early Victorian England, 1830–1865* (1934), ii. 498.
9. Stanley, *Life*, , 285.
10. Ibid. 234.
11. Ibid. 85 and 427; Whitridge, *Dr Arnold of Rugby*, 105–6.
12. Stanley, *Life*, 85; C. H. K. Marten, *On the Teaching of History* (1939), 15.
13. Stanley, *Life*, 291.
14. Whitridge, op. cit. 106; letter to Hawkins, 19 May 1842, full text at Rugby School (only part in Stanley); *The Parents' Review*, Nov. 1895, 839.
15. Marten, op. cit. 14.
16. *Quart. Journ. Ed.* vii, No. XIV (1834), 239; *Misc. Works*, 347; Stanley, *Life*, 80; Fitch, op. cit. 38.
17. *Virtus est bona res*: courage is a good thing; *carpe diem*: enjoy today's fruits; *carpere diem* etc.: The Epicureans bid us enjoy today's fruits; so does Christ.
18. Stanley, *Life*, 473–6.
19. Ibid, 78.
20. *Quart. Journ. Ed*, vii, No. XIV. 242; Fitch, op. cit. 31; Whitridge, op. cit. 104.
21. Stanley, *Life*, 213; Whitridge, op. cit. 127.
22. R. L. Archer, *Secondary Education in the 19th Century* (1921), 36–7; Stanley, *Life*, 80.
23. Ibid. 81; Wymer, *Dr Arnold of Rugby*, 128.
24. Stanley, *Life*, 254.
25. Wymer, op. cit. 130; Stanley, *Life*, 79; F. J. Woodward, *The Doctor's Disciples*, 24.
26. F. J. Woodward, op. cit. 24.
27. Hughes, *Tom Brown's Schooldays*, 181–3. The boy's mistake was to translate the adverb '*triste*' (sorrowfully) as an adjective (*tristis*) agreeing with '*lupus*' (wolf).
28. Wymer, op. cit. 127.

29. Stanley, *Life*, 378; Whitridge, op. cit. 129–30.
30. Wymer, op. cit. 127–8.
31. Stanley, *Life*, 74.
32. Whitridge, op. cit. 131.
33. *Quart. Journ. Ed.* vii, No. XIV. (1834) 236–8; *Misc. Works*, 344–6; Appendix A.
34. Stanley, *Life*, 84–5, 449; Whitridge op. cit. 121 ff.
35. Arnold's predecessor James and Butler, Headmaster of Shrewsbury, had both taught English history in the eighteenth century. *Cambridge History of English Literature*, vol. 12, ch. xiv (1915), 413; J. B. Oldham, *A History of Shrewsbury School* (1952), 92; *Charles Henry Pearson, Memorials*, ed. W. Stebbing (1900), 14–15; E. L. Woodward, *The Age of Reform*, 467.
36. Album in Temple Reading Room, Rugby School.
37. Stanley, *Life*, 389; *Charles Henry Pearson*, 16.
38. Stanley, *Life*, 78–9; *The Leaflet*, edited by members of Rugby School, n.s. vol. iii, No. 9, 100; Whitridge, op. cit. 115–16.
39. *Quart. Journ. Ed.* vii, No. XIV. 242; *Misc. Works*, 351.
40. Bamford, *Thomas Arnold*, 121.
41. Ibid. 117–20; Chandos, *Boys Together*, 248.
42. *Misc. Works*, 232; 423.
43. Stanley, *Life*, 477.
44. Ibid. 276; Whitridge, op. cit. 119–20; Brotherton Lib. F91.
45. Stanley, *Life*, 389.
46. Correlli Barnett, *The Audit of War*, (1986), 214. But cf. Sheldon Rothblatt, 'Ideas of Decline', *London Review of Books* (6–19 Aug. 1981), 13–14; Noel Annan, 'Gentlemen vs. Players', *The New York Review of Books*, vol. xxxv, No. 14, 29 Sept. 1988, 63–9.
47. Mack, op. cit. 143–5; cf. Mark Pattison, *Memoirs*, 237–244.

CHAPTER 6

1. Fitch, *Thomas and Matthew Arnold*, 108.
2. W. C. Lake, *Quarterly Review*, Oct. 1844, 488.
3. Stanley, *Life*, 66.
4. Ibid. 67.
5. Fitch, op. cit. 93.
6. Stanley, *Life*, 68.
7. *Quart. Journ. Ed.* ix, No. XVIII (1835), 287–8; A. C. Percival, *Very Superior Men* (1973), 119; Bamford, *Thomas Arnold on Education*, 129–30.
8. Stanley, *Life*, 70.
9. Ibid. 139. *Propter defectum aetatis*: on account of the weakness of their age.

10. Adamson, *English Education 1789–1902*, 252.
11. Oldham, *A History of Shrewsbury School, 1552–1952*, 97–8.
12. Stanley, *Life*, 68–9.
13. Whitridge, *Dr Arnold of Rugby*, 144.
14. Marten, *On the Teaching of History*, 122.
15. Stanley, *Life*, 69.
16. Archer, *Secondary Education in the 19th Century*, 72.
17. A. Briggs, *Victorian People* (1954), 55–6; Whitridge, op. cit. 124.
18. Sir Francis Doyle, *Reminiscences and Opinions, 1813–1885* (1886), 48.
19. *Quart. Journ. Ed.* ix, No. XVIII (1835), 286; *Misc. Works*, 371.
20. Bamford, *Educational Review*, vol. 10, No. 1 (Nov. 1957), 18–28.
21. The Rt. Hon. Sir Richard Temple, Bt., *The Story of My Life* (1896), Vo. I. 7. In 'roasting', boys were held with their backs close to an open fire so that they became uncomfortably hot and sometimes fainted from the heat.
22. Prothero and Bradley, *Life and Correspondence of Stanley*, I. 40, 47, Wymer, *Dr Arnold of Rugby*, 118.
23. Whitridge, op. cit. 140; G. Melly, *The Experiences of a fag at a Private and a Public School* (1854), 231, 305–6.
24. Bamford, *Thomas Arnold on Education*, 135–6; *Quart. Journ. Ed.* ix, No. XVIII, 286–92; *Misc. Works*, 371–9.
25. Stanley, *Life*, 65–6.
26. Ibid. 67; *Sermons*, v. vii. 55–62.
27. Newsome, *Godliness and Good Learning*, 52.
28. *Sermons* v. vii. 55–62.
29. Stanley, *Life*, 95.
30. Ibid. 139.
31. Ibid. 96–7.
32. Ibid. 66, 136; Chandos, op. cit. 257; Wymer, op. cit. 120.
33. Stanley, *Life*, 136.
34. Wymer, op. cit. 120 (original letter at Rugby School); Cahalin, *A Bibliography of Thomas Arnold*, No. 342, 148.
35. Stanley, *Life*, 49.
36. *Northampton Herald*, 19 Jan. 1836; *John Bull*, 17 Jan. 1836.
37. *Quart. Journ. Ed.*, vol. ix, No. XVIII, 281–86; Whitridge, op. cit, 145; Newsome, op. cit. 52; Fitch, op. cit. 102; Mack, *Public Schools and British Opinion 1780–1860*, 266; *Sermons* iv. xii. 105.
38. *Northampton Herald*, 19 Jan., 2, 23 Feb., 9, 16, 30 Mar. 1833; Bamford, *Thomas Arnold*, 49–53; Newsome, op. cit. 47; Chandos, op. cit. 257–8.
39. Doyle, op. cit. 50; Lake, *Memorials*, 7.
40. Stanley, *Life*, 65.
41. Ibid. 72.

42. Ibid. 48–9.
43. Ibid. 74.
44. Ibid. 71.
45. J. Lindon, letter to Hawkins, 19 Oct. 1837, original in Temple Reading Room at Rugby School.
46. Stanley, *Life*, 72–3.
47. Honey, *Tom Brown's Universe*, 168.
48. Hughes, *Tom Brown's Schooldays*, 177–8.
49. Mack, op. cit. 217; *Quart. Journ. Ed.* x, No. XIX (Apr.–Oct. 1835), 99–100.
50. Stanley, *Life*, 98; Newsome, op. cit. 44.
51. Wymer, op. cit. 118.
52. Rouse, *A History of Rugby School*, 228.
53. Hughes, *Great Public Schools*, ch. xi, 153–4; Fitch, op. cit. 82–3.
54. Clough, *Correspondence*, 59; Fitch, op. cit. 83.
55. Wymer, op. cit. 119.
56. Pell, *Reminiscences*, 40. 'I'm a Rugby scholar and of a Rugby class, And by the wrinkles on my face have tippled many a glass.'
57. Selfe, *Notes on . . . 'Tom Brown's Schooldays'*, 14.
58. Lake, *Memorials*, 17; Newsome, op. cit. 40; Chandos, op. cit. 255.
59. Prothero and Bradley, op. cit., Vol. I, 44, 57.
60. Newsome, op. cit. 197.
61. Hughes, *Fifty Years Ago*, A Layman's Address to Rugby School, Quinquagesima Sunday, 8 Feb. 1891. Cf. Edward C. Mack and W. H. G. Armytage, *Thomas Hughes*, (1952), 24–5.

CHAPTER 7

1. Stanley, *Life*, 140–1.
2. Ibid. 107.
3. Ibid. 40.
4. Ibid. 399.
5. Ibid. 112, 319.
6. Ibid. 141.
7. Ibid. 112.
8. Ibid. 16.
9. Ibid. 39.
10. *Sermons*, ii. v. 32–3, 43.
11. Whitridge, *Dr Arnold of Rugby*, 182.
12. Ibid. 178.
13. Stanley, *Life*, 134.
14. Ibid. 135.
15. Ibid. 158; Whitridge, op. cit. 180.
16. Whitridge, op. cit. 182–3; Stanley, *Life*, 158–9.

17. Whitridge, op. cit. 184–5.
18. Stanley, *Life*, 371–2.
19. Ibid. 371–2.
20. Whitridge, op. cit. 190; Stanley, *Life*, 317.
21. Whitridge, op. cit. 189–90; *John Bull*, 1 Feb. 1835, 2, 17 Jan., 7 Feb., 22 May 1836.
22. Stanley, *Life*, 268–9.
23. Wymer, *Dr Arnold of Rugby*, 167.
24. Ibid. 164.
25. J. B. Mozley, *Essays Historical and Theological*, vol. ii (1878) 37 ff; M. J. Jackson and J. Rogan, Introductory Essay on *Principles of Church Reform* by Thomas Arnold (1962), 70–81; Richard Brent, *Liberal Anglican Politics* (1987), 149; Whitridge, op. cit. 167–8.
26. Whitridge, op. cit. 170–1; T. Mozley, *Reminiscences, chiefly of Oriel College and the Oxford Movement*, vol. ii (1882), 52.
27. *Misc. Works*, 401–24.
28. Stanley, *Life*, 118.
29. Ibid. 159.
30. *Sermons*, ii, Appendix, 279–316.
31. C. R. Moyer, 'The Idea of History in Thomas and Matthew Arnold', *Modern Philology*, 67 (1969–70), 165.
32. Stanley, *Life*, 277.
33. Ibid. 292.
34. Ibid. 112.
35. Ibid. 40–1, 268.
36. Ibid. 24–5.
37. Ibid. 193–4.
38. Ibid. 410.
39. Ibid. 428. On 21 Aug. 1841 he wrote to Dr Hawkins telling him how delighted he was to have accepted Lord Melbourne's offer of the Regius Professorship of Modern History at Oxford.
40. Ibid. 455.
41. Ibid. 113–17.
42. Ibid. 134; Fitch, *Thomas and Matthew Arnold*, 154; Frank M. Turner, *The Greek Heritage in Victorian Britain* (1981), 209–10.
43. Stanley, *Life*, 382.
44. Ibid. 409.
45. Ibid. 115; Trilling, *Matthew Arnold*, 45; G. P. Gooch, *History and Historians in the Nineteenth Century* (2nd edn., 1952), 297–9.
46. Gooch, op. cit. 299.

CHAPTER 8

1. *Educational Analysis*, vol. 1, No. 1 (Summer 1979), 77–9.

2. Stanley, *Life*, viii.
3. Ibid. 142–3.
4. Fitch, *Thomas and Matthew Arnold*, 88–9; Findlay, *Arnold of Rugby*, 124, 130–2, 191.
5. *Sermons*, ii. v. 33–5; ix. 60–1.
6. Selfe, *Notes on . . . 'Tom Brown's Schooldays'*, 22.
7. Prothero and Bradley, *Life and Correspondence of Stanley*, i. 56.
8. Clough, *Correspondence*, 65;
9. Cahalin, *A Bibliography of Thomas Arnold*, no. 57, 82; Letter to Mynors, Brotherton Collection, University of Leeds, Arnold Correspondence, B14239.
10. Wymer, *Dr Arnold of Rugby*, 176.
11. Clough, op. cit. 29–30.
12. *Northampton Herald*, 28 Nov., 26 Dec. 1835; 23 Jan., 23 Apr., 18 June, 9 July, 13 Aug. 1836; *John Bull*, 17 Jan., 7 Feb. 1836; *The Times*, 2 Jan. 1836. Bamford, *Thomas Arnold*, 86, 218.
13. Parents' occupations during Dr Arnold's headmastership, as given in the school Register, were as follows: Esquires 765, Clergymen 247, Aristocracy (including Baronets) 77, Widows 72, Army and Navy 65, Doctors 22, Civil Servants including Foreign Office and Consular 13, Lawyers 5. The figures are approximate because of some overlap.
14. Rouse, *A History of Rugby School*, 196.
15. Bamford, *Thomas Arnold*, 129–30.
16. How to deal with local day boys was a problem in many schools besides Rugby. Cf. John Roach, *A history of secondary education in England, 1800–1870* (1986), 218–25.
17. Bamford, *Thomas Arnold*, 130–40.
18. The *Report* of the House of Lords' Select Committee of 1865 on the Public Schools Bill, 45: 21–2. Mr M. H. Bloxam, a former Foundationer and son of a Rugby master, accused Arnold of so neglecting the Foundationers that they were 'virtually driven away from the school'.
19. Bamford, op. cit. 141; Newsome, *Godliness and Good Learning*, 51.
20. *Report of the Proceeding respecting Rugby School before the Rt. Hon. Lord Langdale, Master of the Rolls, with his Lordship's judgement thereon, 1839*. Cf. *Report* of the House of Lords' Select Committee on the Public Schools Bill (1865), 32–5, 45–6.

CHAPTER 9

1. Whitridge, *Dr Arnold of Rugby*, xxxiv.
2. *Sermons*, v. xxxiv, 340.
3. Selfe, *Notes on . . . 'Tom Brown's Schooldays'*, 29.
4. Stanley, *Life*, 401.

5. Mack, *Public Schools and British Opinion 1780–1860*, 295–6; Whitridge, op. cit. xxxv–xxxvii; Bamford, *Thomas Arnold*, 181.
6. Mack, op. cit. 296; Chandos, *Boys Together*, 262–3.
7. *Memorials of C. H. Pearson*, ed. Stebbing (1900), 17; Mack, op. cit. 297.
8. Whitridge, op. cit. xxxiv; Mack, op. cit. 300.
9. Young, ed., *Early Victorian England, 1830–1865*, 497.
10. Briggs, *Victorian People*, 144.
11. Bamford, *Thomas Arnold*, 172. The obituary was about 250 words long.
12. Fitch, *Thomas and Matthew Arnold*, 155–6.
13. G. G. Bradley, *Recollections of Arthur Penrhyn Stanley* (1883), 22.
14. Ibid. 24; Prothero and Bradley, *Life and Correspondence of Stanley*, i. 41; Lake, *Memorials*, 11.
15. Bradley, op. cit. 30.
16. Ibid. 38; Prothero and Bradley, op. cit. i. 67.
17. Fitch, op. cit. 154; F. J. Woodward, *The Doctor's Disciples*, 41 ff; Prothero and Bradley, op. cit. i. 319–24. A fourth edition was published by Christmas 1844.
18. Bradley, op. cit. 33; Trilling, *Matthew Arnold*, 63; Prothero and Bradley, op. cit. i. 324.
19. Stanley, *Life*, 104–5; Bamford, *Thomas Arnold*, 183–4.
20. C. Wordsworth, *Annals of My Early Life, 1806–1846* (1891), 275–8; J. D'E. Firth, *Winchester College* (1949), 144–5, quoted in T. W. Bamford, *Rise of the Public Schools* (1967), 51–2.
21. Whitridge, op. cit. xliv, xlvi.
22. Mack, op. cit. 234–5.
23. Whitridge, op. cit. 201; S. Butler, *Life of Samuel Butler* (1986), i. 9; Mack, op. cit. 241.
24. Prothero and Bradley, op. cit. i. 78. F. J. Woodward, op. cit. 26
25. Newsome, *Godliness and Good Learning*, 57–8; W. C. Lake, *Quart. Review*, Oct. 1844, 467 ff.
26. Lake, *Memorials*, 11–12; Mack, op. cit. 295.
27. W. P. Ward, *William George Ward and the Oxford Movement*, 107 ff. Newsome, op. cit. 61; Chandos, op. cit. 260, 264.
28. Newsome, op. cit. 59–60.
29. Mack, op. cit. 302.
30. Archer, *Secondary Education in the 19th Century*, 69; Whitridge, op. cit. 201; cf. Phyllis Grosskurth, *The Memoirs of John Addington Symonds* (1984), 87.
31. V. Ogilvie, *The English Public School* (1957), 148, 153, 157; Archer, op. cit. 76; Honey, *Tom Brown's Universe*, 31; D. Newsome, *A History of Wellington College 1859–1959* (1959), 85. The Clarendon Commission, 1861–4, investigated nine public schools: Eton, Win-

chester, Westminster, Charterhouse, St Paul's, Merchant Taylors', Harrow, Rugby, Christ's Hospital.

32. F. J. Woodward, op. cit. 108, 125.
33. Honey, op. cit. 56–64, 68.
34. Newsome, op. cit. *passim*; Archer, op. cit. 74–5.
35. Archer, op. cit. 76 wrongly gives 1843–78; 1842 in Rugby Register.
36. Whitridge, op. cit. 203; Archer, op. cit. 76; F. E. Pollard, ed., *Bootham School, York, 1823–1923*, 44.
37. N. G. Brett-James, *The History of Mill Hill School, 1807–1923* (1924), 139, 173–4.
38. Mack and Armytage, *Thomas Hughes*, 89–90. By 1890 there had been nearly fifty editions or reprints.
39. Trilling, op. cit. 72.
40. Bradley, op. cit. 23; Mack, op. cit. 306; Prothero and Bradley, op. cit. i. 68.
41. I. Quigly, *The Heirs of Tom Brown* (1982), 61.
42. *Conference and Common Room*, vol. 20, No. 2, 5–7; Mack and Armytage, op. cit. 96. Hughes emphasized the Doctor's forthright, vigorous, and kindly traits.
43. W. M. Payne, *The Dial*, vol. 24 (1898), 115, quotes Matthew Arnold's view of *Tom Brown's Schooldays*: 'it gives only one side, and that not the best side of Rugby School life, or of Arnold's character. . . . Hughes' own boyhood . . . not spent with the best set at Rugby'.
44. Marten, *On the Teaching of History*, 147–8.
45. Fitch, op. cit. 104–6; Arbuthnot, *Memories of Rugby and India*, 48.
46. Hughes, *Fifty Years Ago*, A Layman's Address to Rugby School, Quinquagesima Sunday, 8 Feb, 1891.
47. Mack and Armytage, op. cit. 24–5.
48. Wymer, *Dr Arnold of Rugby*, 198–9.
49. Fitch, op. cit. 152–3; Mack, op. cit. 293; Wymer, op. cit. 199.
50. Fitch, op. cit. 154–5.

CHAPTER 10

1. Percival, *Very Superior Men*, 122–3.
2. Chandos, *Boys Together*, 247.
3. Mack and Armytage, *Thomas Hughes*, 101. *Times Literary Supplement*, 13 June 1942, 291: 'The two bases of Arnold's method—school Chapel the centre of school life and the sixth form the main instrument of government—have led to [the] alienation of public schoolboys from real religion, and to the cults of athleticism and "good form". The fault lay with his successors who were unable to reinterpret his ideal, and adapt his methods.
4. Adamson, *English Education 1789–1902*, 67.

5. Whitridge, *Dr Arnold of Rugby*, xli.
6. Bamford, *Thomas Arnold*, 188–9.
7. Bradfield (1850), Cheltenham (1841), Clifton (1862), Haileybury (1862), Lancing (1848), Marlborough (1843), Radley (1847), Rossall (1844), Wellington (1859).
8. Whitridge, op. cit. xlix; Newsome, *A History of Wellington College, 1859–1959* (1959), 4.
9. Whitridge, op. cit. xxxix.
10. Ibid. xli-xliii.
11. Ibid. 1, 213.
12. Ibid. xlv.
13. Stanley, *Life*, 233.
14. Whitridge, op. cit. 209.
15. Ibid. 211.
16. Trilling, *Matthew Arnold*, 76; cf. Bamford, *Thomas Arnold on Education*, 4.
17. Fitch, *Thomas and Matthew Arnold*, 108.
18. Chandos, op. cit. 265–6. Cf. ch. 6, note 61.
19. Whitridge, op. cit. xiv–xvii. Cf. Sir Michael Sadler, *Times Educational Supplement*, 13 June 1942: 'Thomas Arnold ranks among the great statesmen of the first half of the nineteenth century. . . . Patriot, social reformer, historian, divine . . . above all else a prophet—a forth teller of what he believed to be the truth.'
20. William Golding, 'Headmasters', The *Spectator*, No. 6894, 12 Aug. 1960, 252–3.

INDEX